Down The Road In Thailand, Cambodia And Vietnam

Tim and Cindie Travis

Down The Road In Thailand, Cambodia And Vietnam

"A Bicycle Tour Through War, Genocide And Forgiveness"

Down The Road Publishing

Greenwood, Indiana

Down The Road In Thailand, Cambodia And Vietnam
A Bicycle Tour Through War, Genocide And Forgiveness.
By Tim & Cindie Travis

Published by:
Down The Road Publications LLC
973 Sleepy Hollow Ct.
Greenwood, IN 46142
http://DownTheRoad.org/Publishing/

Copyright © 2010 by Tim Travis
ISBN 978-0-9754427-6-0
Library of Congress Control Number: 2010923302

Photo Credit: All photographs taken by Tim or Cindie Travis except photo at Smiley's Guesthouse, Siem Reap, Cambodia taken by David Munusamy.

Acknowledgement

We would like to acknowledge both of our families in the USA who have supported our crazy desire to see the world on bicycles in many ways. Without their assistance the story of our journey would have never made it to print.

We would also like to thank the following people for their technical assistance in completing this sometimes difficult project. Megan Reed, Alan Wechsler, Carol Baldwin and Carolyn Travis.

Table of Contents

Map of Southeast Asia

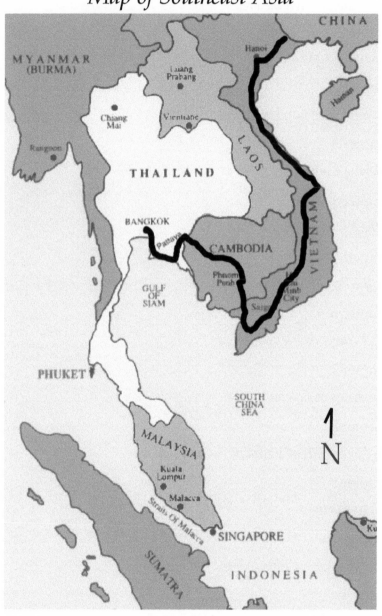

—— Our route through the area

Chapter 1
Something Called Freedom

Tim and Cindie Travis

Freedom is addictive. Too much of it, and there's no turning back. Cindie and I found that out for ourselves after two years on the road – cycling from our home in Arizona to the southern region of South America.

When we first started our journey on March 30, 2002, we set out on what we thought was going to be a seven-year cycling adventure. That's how much time we could afford, based on the amount of money we had saved up after living frugally for nearly five years before we left. And once the money ran out, we reckoned ... well, it was back to our home, back to our working lives.

Then came this freedom thing. We got a taste. We wanted more.

During our two years on the road, our views of the world changed. We went from being Arizona residents who liked to travel, to travelers whose only home was on the back of our bikes. We proved to naysayers – who thought we would miss the comforts of home, or get killed in a distant land – that we could not only do it, but also have the time of our lives in the process.

After our two years in Latin America ended, we returned to relatives in Indiana for a short break to take stock in our finances and decide our next move. Our bank accounts were getting low. Freedom beckoned, then reality intruded. How could we continue our bike ride forever and never run out of money?

And we thought we found a way.

In Argentina, I wrote a book. It was called *The Road That Has No End*, and it explored our decision to ride around the world, and the first year of cycling from Prescott, Arizona to Panama City, Panama in Central America. Later, I wrote a second book, *Down the Road in South America* that described our second year of cycling in South America. Although these books are sequential, it is not necessary to read the first two to understand and enjoy this one. Information about all our books can be found on our web site, www.DownTheRoad.org.

I wrote these books despite being dyslexic. Dyslexia is something I've had my entire life, and is the reason I chose a career in Special Education – to help others with the same problem. Thanks to a patient wife and a computer that checks spelling and reads text out loud, I became an author, which was a possibility that only a few years earlier I never would have dared imagine. It gave me confidence; made me realize I could do (nearly) whatever I set my mind to.

Starting a business and self-publishing books was an incredible learning experience. The first book took months of work. We had to hire a professional editor, a cover artist and a commercial printer. We learned how to edit photographs, and lay out the book with text, images and everything else.

And then, in order to keep riding while selling the books, we had to learn about the "fulfillment" industry. We found a company that stored our books, took orders from our web site, mailed them out and kept various retail stores stocked. We also had to learn to use complicated accounting software that would track sales and other income so we could pay all the applicable taxes.

By the time we reached Asia, our business was earning about half our daily expenses through book sales and pay per click advertising on our web site. It wasn't a lot, but it was a start and showed potential. The number of site visitors was growing - sometimes doubling in one month - thanks to the thousands of folks who found us through search engines, subscribed to our email list, and passed our stories on to friends.

Girls riding their bikes to school.

The bicycle is the workhorse of Southeast Asia.

Cambodian woman at the market.

Buddhist Temples in Thailand have beautiful decorations.

5

Tim's loaded touring bike.

We also attracted a few sponsorships which helped cut down on expenses. Ortlieb, the German-based manufacturer of high-end cycling panniers, offered us two full sets of their excellent waterproof bags. Phil Wood Co., maker of the world's best bicycle hubs and more, gave us two sets of sealed hubs - just before I was about to buy these things myself. Koga USA, the American arm of the Dutch maker of touring bicycles, offered two bikes at wholesale cost and the mechanism to refer customers from our web site and earn commission sales.

After two years of hard work as nobodies, it seemed we were finally being discovered by the cycling world.

Our original plan after spending time in Indiana was to head to Africa. However, the dollar was doing better in Asia, expenses were less there and Cindie found a great deal on a pair of one-way tickets to Bangkok. So Asia it was.

As we prepared to ship out to Thailand on Nov. 22, 2004 we really had no idea if our plan would work. This new way of living would require us to run our business from our saddles – using our laptop for what others do in an office, and checking in when we were in towns large enough to have Internet access, hard to find in rural Southeast Asia.

We were cycling entrepreneurs; early pioneers in international travel telecommuting and only time would tell if our business plan would work. The catch was all of our business endeavors had to pan out. We had less money for traveling now that we had invested in a book. Would our book pay off? How long would it take to get our investment back and break even with our monthly expenses? We had no idea. If we succeeded we could travel indefinitely. If we failed we would fall flat on our faces and have to go home and look for jobs sooner than expected.

And were we ready for Asia? We didn't know that either, but figured we'd find out soon. After two years on the road, we had suffered through mechanical problems, exhaustion, learning a foreign language, dangerous traffic, crime, poverty, illnesses and culture shock. We felt like grizzled, cycle-touring veterans. I was 38 years old; my wife 43. It was six years since we biked up to a drive-thru wedding chapel in Las Vegas, said our vows and rode away on a tandem bike.

I promised Cindie that life together wouldn't be boring.

And it certainly hasn't been. Asia would be different from our time in Latin America. There would be multiple languages, most of which we wouldn't have a chance of understanding, plus an entirely foreign alphabet. The customs and religions would be completely different to what we had grown up with. We would be eating mysterious foods. Smelling exotic scents. And it would mean a new and intimidating distance from home - halfway around the world from America and our families.

We were nervous, but there was no point in stopping now. We were addicted to freedom and financially committed. And the only cure was the road that has no end.

Cambodian driving a homemade cart.

Chapter 2
Thailand: The Land of Smiles

Tim and Cindie Travis in front of a Buddhist Wat.

It took 27 hours to fly from Indianapolis, in the heart of the United States Midwest, to Bangkok, Thailand. We had come so far – after more than two years on bicycles, we were finally crossing into the other side of the world. It was Nov. 22, 2004.

Our digital wristwatches read noon. The local time was midnight. Clearly, we had some catching up to do.

The first job was getting out of the Bangkok airport. It was a heady experience. Dizzy from lack of sleep, our bodies stiff from too many hours on an airplane, we followed our fellow passengers through customs – easily passing through the checkpoint, where an officer merely glanced at our passports while stamping in a free 30-day tourist visa.

And then we were in. We loaded our boxed bikes and bags onto a free luggage cart (only western countries seem to have the audacity to charge a new arrival to the country for a luggage cart) and wandered through the security doors. Suddenly we were outside in the warm, humid air. Where were the duty-free shops, the fast-food restaurants, the bookstores and clothing stores? There was nothing to this airport but a few money-change booths, some food stalls and masses and masses of people.

Then we saw the line for the taxi. There were a hundred little yellow taxis in line, with a hundred new arrivals waiting for them. None of them seemed big enough to fit our bikes.

Finally, we found someone with a van who could take our stuff and ourselves downtown. After an hour of buzzing through traffic, we arrived at our hotel and collapsed into bed, exhausted but far too wired to sleep.

At our hotel, where the manager offers a "wai" (a bow of respect) before the Buddhist shrine when he arrives for work in the morning, we put our bikes together and tried to take stock of our new home. It was not easy. Only a day earlier (actually two days, thanks to the International Date Line) we had been with our families in the United States. And a few weeks before that we had spent several years riding through Central and South America, where we learned a new language and transformed our lives from bicycle tourists to professional bike travelers.

And now we were on a new continent ready to start the

Statue of Buddha at Wat Pho.

next chapter of our journey. All we had to do was adjust to the new time zone, and the new culture.

Quite a frenetic culture. Bangkok is a large city of nine million people, 500 Buddha statues and centuries of history. It is located in the bulging center of Thailand, a mix of ancient and modern, where barefoot monks carrying donation bowls walk down the street as modern businessmen zoom past in

Buddhist Wat along the Chao Phraya river.

Bangkok, Thailand. Our first look at driving on the left.

air-conditioned sports cars (or at least they would zoom if the glut of Asian metropolis traffic would let them).

We discovered the first step was communication as we braved our first visit to a restaurant. In an effort to find a place cheaper than the standard tourist fare, we left the tourist district to find a restaurant frequented by locals.

"How much" we asked at the door. We were met with blank stares.

"¿Cuanto Cuesta?" I asked in my best Spanish. Now the Thai face behind the counter was even more confused.

Our first lesson: Spanish was no good here. It would take us a few days to get out of the habit of speaking what had been our most recent language.

Once we got over our initial travel exhaustion, we began to explore the city. We made excursions to the king's palace and – as unimpressive as it may sound - the royal barge museum. Those ancient barges, opulent long boats rowed by men, transported royalty and in ancient times were used for river and sea battles. Every space was decorated with detailed carvings covered in gold leaf and imitation rubies.

Thais love their royal family, both past and present. Billboard portraits of the current King, Queen, or both can be seen everywhere, from highways to country roads.

We also visited several Buddhist temples or "Wats." Wats consist of groups of beautifully decorated buildings with ornate statues of Buddhas sitting, standing or reclining. Buddhist monks, with shaved heads and orange robes, sit medi-

Decorated boat at Royal Barge Museum.

Business men and monks at a ceremony.

tating or chanting. They live a simple life devoted to study and prayer, with few personal possessions.

It was our first experience with a religion other than Christianity. We knew little about it, however its doctrine of nonviolence and peacefulness is certainly appealing. We would have plenty of time to learn more.

We rode the water taxis along the Chao Phraya River and saw the floating market, where farmers sell their wares from boats floating in backwater canals. We spent time on the tourist street of Khao San Road, home to cheap drinks, cheap hotels, cheap Internet, cheap clothes and cheap prostitutes. And we wandered down streets where tourists never tread, looking to find our way into this foreign culture. The Thais call Bangkok Krung Thep, Krung Thep means "City of Angels." It had many secrets, and we would only become privy to a few of them.

After a few days, it was time to leave Bangkok. But how? There's no grid here, and the roads are a confusing tangle choked with traffic. How would we get out without getting mowed down by a bus or poisoned by carbon monoxide?

Fortunately, we had a friend. Before we left, a Thai couple - (Wan and Mou), who are traveling by bicycle around the world - had introduced us via email to a 25-year-old Bangkok resident, an avid cyclist named Yu. He worked for a company that leads foreigners on bike trips in Thailand. The company was called Spice Roads.

"Mr. Tim," he wrote in an email, "I would be happy to show you and your wife how to get out of Bangkok by bike."

15

Yu had taught himself English only six years earlier. Thanks to practice with tourists, he was proficient. We called his cell phone and he answered while biking through Bangkok's congested traffic. We could hear the horns and throbbing motors over the phone, and could barely imagine him riding one-handed while talking on the cell phone. He was happy to hear from us, and told us he'd meet us at our hotel.

When he came to our first meeting, we recognized him immediately - he wore bike gloves, shorts, bike shoes and carried a detached handlebar bag under his arm. His legs bore the knotted muscles of a man who has seen many kilometers on a saddle.

We immediately felt at home sitting down with a fellow cyclist, even one with a heavy accent from a culture we barely knew. Cycling is a sport that transcends international boundaries.

In truth, Yu reminded us of the way we were before we left on our trip. He told us: "Some day I will take my own bicycle tour around the world." And we believed him.

Yu took us to a top end bike shop called Probike. Amazingly, even across the globe in a small Asian nation, we could find a store that offered qualified bike mechanics and enough gear to keep Lance Armstrong riding smoothly.

The next morning, he met us at our hotel to lead us on the first day of our two-wheeled journey. Our job was to remember which side of the road to ride on – Thais, like Brits, Indians and Australians, drive on the left, not the right.

Buddhist monk at Wat Pho.

Cindie and Yu, our guide out of Bangkok.

Cindie in Bangkok traffic.

As we rolled out of the hotel lobby– out of shape, over-weight, but with new Ortlieb bags and newly-tuned bikes that were ready for anything - I kept repeating "stay to the left, stay to the left" in my head. I heard Cindie, behind me, actually saying it out loud.

When we came to the first intersection I instinctively looked to the left, saw that it was clear and went for it, and nearly got hit. In this country, traffic comes from the right when crossing streets. I made a mental note. A mistake like that would cut our trip short very quickly.

Without Yu, we might never have left Bangkok. Like many big Asian cities Bangkok is not a bicycle-friendly place. Roads are choked with cars, tuk tuks (three-wheeled enclosed mo-torbikes) and an infinite number of motor scooters, all belch-ing black exhaust and buzzing like ten thousand petrol-burn-ing bees. And unlike in the United States, where vehicles are separated neatly by white lines, there were no road markers to keep us even slightly safe. Here, every stretch of the road is fair game, and any space not occupied by cars or trucks will be filled by smaller vehicles.

At the front of every stoplight, noisy scooters surrounded us, jockeying for position. Many of them held three, even four family members. The father drove–usually talking on a cell phone - while the mother sat side-saddle behind him, one or two children sitting on her lap.

Everyone in Bangkok talks on the phone while driving. Even Yu's phone rang several times as he led us down the busy road. He had an elaborate system of using his shoulder

19

and neck so he could steer, shift, brake, and talk in rapid-fire Thai, all at the same time.

We felt left behind in this high-tech world – after all, we were from what was ostensibly the most technologically-advanced country in the world, and we didn't have a cell phone. Though, we also felt a lot safer with both hands on our handlebars.

Yu took us 50 kilometers (31 miles) in the next three hours, always heading to the southeast. Eventually, we stopped to eat at an open-air restaurant.

"Are we still in Bangkok?" I asked our guide. The roads were just as congested, the surroundings just as urban-looking.

Yu laughed. "Mr. Tim," he said, "we left Bangkok two hours ago."

The industrial outskirts of the city seemed to go on forever. It was time for a rest. We sat down on several cheap plastic chairs – they're ubiquitous in Asia – and Yu told us some do's and don'ts about Thai customs.

First thing to remember: don't insult the King. And that wasn't a joke. We realized how serious he was when, in reading our guidebook later, we read about a Thai intellectual who was arrested in 1991 for making a passing reference to the king's "interest in yachting." A few years later, he was arrested again for referring to the royal family as "ordinary people."

No insults to the king. Considering we didn't even know

his name, we figured that wouldn't be too hard.

Other things to keep in mind: wear conservative clothes in the temples; remember to wai back to a person who wais to you (unless it is a child or a waiter) if your not sure the best thing to do is smile back; don't point with your fingers or the sole of your foot; don't touch a Thai on the head and never shake hands or pass money with the left hand (which the Thais use for wiping after the toilet). Especially for Cindie, don't touch the monks, as they are not supposed to make contact with women.

We also had to remember to take off our shoes every time we entered a person's home and to never step over a person who was lying on the ground, even if they were in the middle of the sidewalk. It was also important, when visiting, to eat any food put down in front of us, no matter what it looked like. At the time, this rule didn't mean much to us. It was only later, when we realized that both insects and reptiles factor into the Southeast Asian cuisine, that we realized what we were in for.

Clearly there would be a lot of things for us to keep in mind as we made our way into a part of Thailand where "farangs" (Westerners) rarely tread. We hoped we would remember everything.

"Don't worry, Mr. Tim," Yu said, smiling. "You will do very well in my country."

He gave us a final wai, then hopped on his bike and pedaled back toward Bangkok. And there went our first friend

Cindie waiting for a monk to cross the street.

in Thailand. We watched him disappear amid the traffic, wondering how we would survive without a guide in such a foreign place.

One crank revolution at a time, that is how. We climbed back onto our bikes and headed back into traffic, thinking that one of the downsides about our life on two wheels was always saying good-bye.

Less than five minutes later, I got my first flat.

I rode over a sliver of metal that pushed about three centimeters (one inch) into my tire. It was hauntingly like our first day out of Prescott, Arizona. Darn. I pushed my bike under the shade of a nearby furniture store and began the task of locating all of the tools that we had hastily packed the night before.

And then we had company – and our second friend in Thailand. A salesman from the furniture shop, anticipating my problem, brought me a pair of needle-nose pliers to pull out the metal thorn. I looked up the Thai word for "thank you" in our phrase book – "khawp khun" - but pronounced it so poorly I had to show him the book.

Thai, like other Southeast Asian languages, is tonal – the tone of the word is as important as the word itself. The salesman gave us a quick language lesson and then we were back on the road, struggling through the hottest part of the day.

Later, we rode into the town of Chonburi. Our first destination outside Bangkok was supposed to have several hotels. However, we couldn't read Thai, and few signs were in English.

Hmm. We looked at the squiggles of Thai script and were completely lost. How could we ask the thousands of people milling around us on this busy street corner? First, we looked up the word "hotel" and "please" in our phrase book but no one understood our bad (or off-tone) pronunciation.

Next, we tried to memorize the first few characters of

Red Cross sign, in Thai script.

"hotel" in Thai script. Thai letters are completely different than the Latin alphabet, full of spirals and hooks and arches – more like musical notes than letters.

Finally, I resorted to showing the word "hotel" in our phrase book to people, underlining the word with the edge of a business card so they knew which word we were looking for. They offered an expression of nurturing concern (perhaps for our sanity), and pointed down the road. After riding a bit longer, we saw the word "hotel" on a sign in English. Yes!

Now we were on familiar ground. I stayed with the bikes while Cindie went in to secure us a room. After saying hello in Thai to the clerk, she pointed at different words and numbers in our phrase book to agree on a room and a price. The hotel staff helped us one at a time into the elevator with our bike and we were set for the night.

That phrase book would become one of our most valuable possessions. It covered the seven or so languages we'd encounter in Southeast Asia. Starting out, we had no idea how useful it would become – and how much we would be relying on it.

From Chonburi we rode to our first Thai beach, Pattaya and then onto Ko Samet National Park. We arrived in Pattaya in the late afternoon ready to pass out from the heat. We were still not use to the high temperature and humidity of tropical Thailand. In late afternoon it was over 90° F (32°C) with over 80% humidity. Our bodies were still use to the cool November climate in Indiana where it was only 50 ° F (10° C). No matter how much sweat poured off of me I still couldn't cool off.

This city is a world-famous beach, popular with tourists both Asian and Western. While it has plenty of family entertainment, its biggest fame comes from X-rated services. Men come from around the world to partake in its hundreds of strip-joints, far more extreme than anything seen in the United States, and a wide range of prostitutes (mostly women, but also men and "lady boys."). No doubt some of the seedier places also included underage workers as well.

Accommodations range from backpacker standard fare to five star hotels. Pattaya has a real party atmosphere with streets lined with bars and outdoor patios filled with girls waiting to talk to anyone who strolled their way. I went out with a couple of English guys for the evening while Cindie

The beach at Pattaya.

The girls of Pattaya waiting for the party to begin.

went for a traditional Thai massage. That night as we went from bar to bar I heard, "Buy me a drink, Mr." more times than I can remember. I really wanted to see what the attraction to this area was all about, I was not interested in sex, I had a wife down the street getting a traditional massage.

On our second night in town we decided to eat at the local outdoor market. While eating our Pad Thai (spicy rice noodles), a Swedish man sat down at our table. The first thing we noticed was how pale and sickly he looked.

Cindie asked him: "Are you feeling alright?"

"No, not so nice" he said. "I have a touch of malaria; I got malaria when I was in Africa a few years back..."

We talked about Africa and his travels over the next hour or so and then he left. After he was gone, I said to Cindie, "Well, I guess we'd better start taking our antimalaria pills before we enter Cambodia. Otherwise we'll end up looking like that guy."

"I'm not sure it was malaria that made him look bad," she said. "I think he has some other serious disease."

We never found out what he had, but this would not be the last we saw of this Swede.

Ko Samet National Park is an island and required a boat ride to reach. We wheeled the heavy bikes aboard via a wooden ramp, and made ready to relax.

On the island, we kicked back in a tropical paradise. We removed our bags and went on a long mountain-bike ride across the island. On the way back to the mainland the boat

Tim loading his bike on the boat to Ko Samet.

Our bikes on the boat.

was smaller than the one we took out. It didn't have a wooden ramp, so our bikes had to be loaded over the side of the boat. As my bike was being passed over, a gust of wind hit the heavy boat and pushed it away from land. My bike was hanging over the ocean and the heavy boat was slowly going out to sea. Adrenaline suddenly surging, I quickly yanked my two-wheeled rig back on the dock.

That was close. Hauling my bike out of the salt water wasn't exactly the kind of fishing I had in mind on our trip.

One thing we learned quickly is that Thailand deserved its reputation as the "Land of Smiles."

Thais have an unstoppable sense of humor. They love a good joke. For example, while waiting at a red light with the usual pack of motor scooters, I like to pretend that I can't start my imaginary bicycle engine. They jokingly offer me tools or pretend to push-start me. They laugh so hard that they miss the light change.

That just confirmed what we had already learned on *The Road that Has No End*. No matter what culture you are from – no matter how different skin colors, languages, beliefs – we all want the same thing. Parents want their children to grow up with the best opportunities; teachers want their students to learn; workers want the work-day to end. And everyone admires honesty, and a job well done. These similarities are the language we all speak and the only language I had to communicate with ... at least until I learned more Thai.

Another thing we learned is how good the food of Thailand is. The country enjoys a reputation as having one of the world's great cuisines, and after several years of eating stringy meats and bland rice and beans throughout South America we quickly agreed. For me the only close competitors are the fantastic steaks in Argentina and the great traditional Mexican dishes.

Here you could get delicious Pad Thai on the street for the value of two American quarters, and delicious curries in yellow, red or green, with the freshest fish or chicken or squid you could ever ask for. Fantastic – so long as you had a good stomach for spicy food. If not, you would always be served enough rice to (eventually) blot out the pain of too many hot peppers.

We soon settled into a routine of waking up at 5 a.m. and hitting the road by 7 a.m. leaving early gave us a few hours for riding in the coolness of the morning. By the time 11 a.m. arrived the street venders started cooking lunch. The variety of smells and textures of Thai food are dazzling, and we would stop several times to eat throughout the day.

During an overnight stop in Klaeng a few nights later we got a surprise about the variety of Thai cuisine.

We had already secured a room and were on the street at a large sidewalk restaurant. Cindie, always the first of our duo to try something new, liked a dish our neighbor was eating: a reddish meat that looked to be peppered or otherwise covered in seasonings. Because we did not speak any Thai yet, she ordered it by pointing at the neighbor's plate – after all, it looked good, didn't it?

Cindie eating Pad Thai, spicy noodles with pork and bean sprouts.

I had my normal, safe Pad Thai, while Cindie tried her mysterious, reddish meat. I tried a spoonful from the small, stone pot in which it was served – not bad, I agreed.

When it was time to order seconds I walked up to the

31

Which meat would you pick?

counter to order another pot of the meat. However, first I had
to know what to ask for. I pulled out our trusty phrase book,
pointed to the stove – filled with simmering pots and pans
– and then showed her the page with the words for "pork,"

"beef" and "chicken."

I could tell that she understood my question but could not find the answer in my book.

I rephrased my question. I pointed at the pot. "Mooo?" I asked.

The lady shook her head.

"Oink, Oink?" I asked, somewhat tentatively.

She shook her head again and made a strange sound: "Hrrrr, hrrrr."

Huh? Now it was my time to look confused.

She repeated the sound again. And scraped her foot on the ground. Like a horse clawing the ground with its hoof.

A horse. That's what we were eating.

I ordered more Pad Thai.

Cindie, from our plastic table at the curb, had seen the whole exchange. "Tim, please tell me that I did not just eat a horse," she begged.

"I doubt it was a whole horse," I replied. "That would feed a hundred people."

"Oh, God," Cindie said, looking down at her plate in disgust. Cindie loves horses.

"Don't worry," I added. "It probably wasn't a race horse. It obviously wasn't very fast."

Cindie, who grew up working in a horse stable, looked sick. My Pad Thai was delivered. I gave the lady an "oink, oink" and thumbs up just to double check that the meat in my noodles was pig, not horse. The lady oinked back, which

Street vendor making our dinner.

Thais have a wide selection of food to choose from.

we took to mean either "yes" or "I'd better humor the weird Farangs before they cause more trouble."

From that day on, whenever we rode past a horse pulling a plow or wagon I would mimic "Hrrr hrrr" and remind Cindie of the day she ate Seabiscuit.

We also learned to be more careful before ordering. Soon after, we saw a street vender selling such delicacies as fried maggots and cockroaches. I was glad that they were recognizable by shape – I had no idea how to mimic the sound of a cockroach.

Our next stop was Chantaburi, one of the world's most important gem-trading cities. Cindie was thrilled. She's a geologist, so she's naturally drawn to shiny and glittery rocks. More than 60 percent of the world's rubies pass through a few blocks of this city. Clearly we had to stop and poke around.

"But no buying," I warned my wife, who quietly agreed.

We spent two days resting in town and wandered around bazaars where piles of expensive gemstones were bought and sold. Cindie was as good as her word. It must have been hard for her to walk past such alluring piles of red, green and yellow stones. Gems and bikes don't mix well.

From there, we rode over some low-lying mountains before reaching the Thai/Cambodian border. At the start of the first climb, we expected it to be like the mountains we had grown used to in the Andes. We settled into listening to music on our mp3 player and spinning on our bikes to the top. We needn't have bothered.

Gem Trading Market: I think the offer was to low for the seller.

Gems, being sorted and weighted.

In the Andes, climbs went on for as long as several days as we gained and lost thousands and thousands of feet, climbing through various ecosystems and numerous levels of pain and exhaustion.

However, that was Latin America. In Thailand the climb lasted less than two hours and was practically painless. We arrived at Aranya Prathet and the Cambodian border and made preparations to enter the undeveloped and war-torn country of Cambodia.

This would be the true test. Thailand has divided highways, air-conditioned buses, 7-11 convenience stores and (occasionally) flush toilets. Cambodia had bad roads, land mines, widespread poverty and the memory of the Khmer Rouge, one of the most despised and repressive governments in modern history.

It was time to keep turning the cranks, and see what was around the next bend in the road.

When we looked closer we realized these platters displayed cooked cockroaches, maggots and grubs.

A close up of grubs and onions.

Chapter 3
Entering Cambodia

Cindie at the hazy border between Thailand and Cambodia.

We noticed the difference even before we were over the border. After we passed through the Thai exit point (and the sign warning of a death penalty to anyone who was caught possessing illegal drugs), we saw the Cambodians.

They were lining up by the hundreds to pass from Cambodia into Thailand, the Southeast Asian equivalent of Mexicans waiting at Tijuana to pass into the United States. Quietly and patiently they stood in the morning heat; the men wearing T-shirts and shorts, the women in long-sleeved clothes

I watch the bikes while Cindie gets our entry stamps into Cambodia.

and wicker hats, some with faces covered by a cloth balaclava also known as a krama. In this culture, light skin is considered to be of a higher class than darker skin, which can come from laboring in the hot rice paddies or doing dusty roadwork. Thus the women endeavor to prevent getting a suntan, despite the obvious discomfort.

We couldn't help but be conscious of our bicycles, and the wealth contained in our panniers.

As we waited for our entry stamps, I thought back to all the preparations we had made to come here. For instance, there was the Doxycycline, our daily orange antibiotic pill that would ward off Malaria. We had stocked up on all necessary supplies, such as easy-to-prepare noodles and vegetables. We've learned that things available in one country may be unheard of across the border.

We had made careful count of our money, and with the shrinking value of the dollar we were glad we had picked Asia for our next destination after Latin America. One of the biggest expenses seemed to be visas. Cambodia, for instance, cost US $30 for 30 days each, a noticeable percentage of our daily budget.

This was our thirteenth border crossing. A lot can be learned about two countries by the activities at the border. Usually the poorer country has many things for sale so their better off neighbor can avoid high taxes and buy cheap goods. Cambodia was no exception.

This border was chaotic. Well-dressed Thais in new Toyota Camrys parked in guarded lots and walked across the border to shop and gamble in Cambodia. The border was only a few hours drive from Bangkok, and the casinos in the cross-border "No-Man's Land" looked new and transplanted from somewhere else.

The casinos were the only structures that looked modern. Everything else, including the people, looked worn out.

As I waited for Cindie, I found out the Cambodians were streaming into Thailand on day-long work passes. There were carts and wagons of all style. Small motor scooters pulled trailers full of people, the two-stroke engines laboring under the weight. There were old farm wagons made entirely out of wood, including the wheels, which were pulled by water

Hand cranked cart used by an amputee, most likely from stepping on a land mine.

buffalo and oxen. In some ways, life hadn't changed here in centuries.

In the rag-tag line of squeaky carts were several which were propelled by a hand crank. Another symbol of Cambodia's sad past. The country still had millions of land-mines hidden in rice paddies and along mountain paths. The men who drove these hand-powered carts had no legs – blown off by mines, no doubt. It's the gift of war that keeps on giving.

I watched our loaded bikes while Cindie waited in line

and arranged the entry stamps in our passports. All I could do was sit as thousands of forgotten members of humanity passed before me. For them, life was hard and a struggle merely to survive.

It was difficult to imagine what they thought of us. My life seemed so safe by comparison. Here, anyone over 30 had seen and experienced more than most Westerners could ever imagine.

I'm sure they wondered what business we had as tourists here, cycling practically care-free past their difficult lives. Then Cindie emerged, triumphantly clutching our passports with our 30-day visa approved. It was time to find out for ourselves.

It's impossible to talk about Cambodia without talking about Pol Pot. The reviled communist leader reached the height of his power in 1975. As the world focused on nearby Vietnam, Pol Pot changed the name of Cambodia to Kampuchea and declared that the country would now begin "Year Zero" of its new history. The cities were emptied, and the entire population forced to live on large farms. This was progress to the Khmer Rouge.

Meanwhile, Pol Pot began to "cleanse" the population of anyone he deemed guilty of interfering with his new history. That included anybody who had been educated: monks, teachers, doctors, engineers, politicians and even people with the bad luck of having to wear glasses.

Those who weren't executed fared only a little better. They

Tim riding past a water buffalo cart.

A huge billboard seen from the road: "We no Longer Need Weapons".

were fed a starvation diet of rice and forced to labor on collective farms. In all, about two million people – a fifth of the population – were killed until 1979, when Vietnam invaded the country and Pol Pot fled to the far mountains. There, he lived for nearly two decades before being captured and dying under house arrest.

It would take the country years to recover from this forced disaster. Years to dig up the bones of the killing fields, to dig out the land mines, to prosecute – or forgive – the men who committed these crimes and continue to live among them.

Yet in the past few years Cambodia has seen an incredible transformation. Take Angkor Wat, the world-famous temple site that would be our first destination. A few years ago, very few tourists came here, and those that did risked land-mines and violence from armed locals.

Today Seam Reap, the city next to the complex, sees a million tourists a year. It has its own international airport and five-star hotels. Even the New York Times Travel Section saw fit to write a "24 hours in..." story about the city, a sure sign of success.

Every day, thousands of Cambodians from nearby villages commute into the city to work in the hospitality and tourism industry. They walk or bike past large billboards depicting a US made M-16 military rifle broken in half. The caption, in Khmer and English, insists: "We no Longer Need Weapons." Clearly, it was a new era we were about to pedal into.

Riding those first few kilometers through the rough and dirty border town in an isolated region of Cambodia was a jolt to our senses.

The first thing I noticed was the smell of fish guts rotting in the sun. I soon learned while riding I can hold my breath for a full minute if I had too.

The vehicles on the road looked straight out of a Dr. Seuss children's book. We rode past old trucks, some lacking an engine hood, others lacking doors, or some without roofs. Their beds were overloaded with goods or people, and the vehicles crawled slowly down the rough road like overburdened beasts, which they were, I suppose.

Faster moving motor-scooters carried dozens of squawking ducks hanging by their feet. Indeed, we passed some large duck farms as we rode through the pancake-flat countryside.

The road soon turned to dirt, with deep potholes – kettle holes, more like it—and deep fissures in the roadbed carved by heavy rain. There were long stretches with unbearable dust. The krama scarf that Cambodians wear serves as both dust filter and hat. These scarves were common and a source of ethnic Khmer (Cambodian) identity. When the dust was thick, heads would be completely covered with fabric. I wished we had some.

Houses were nothing more than thatched rooms on stilts above a squalid swamp. Trash collection was nonexistent—garbage was routinely raked together and burned every few meters. We pedaled through a blur of black smoke from burning plastic.

Krama scarfs worn by Cambodians.

Every so often locals sold beverages – canned beer, Red Bull or juice in cardboard bricks – on the side of the road. The drinks were in coolers but there was no ice in them. I passed on the warm beer.

In other spots, men sold gasoline stored in liter-size plastic bottles, which glowed yellow in the morning sun. Considering how many people smoke around here, it's a wonder there are not more filling station disasters.

Typical house on stilts in Cambodia.

Traveling salesman selling housewares in small villages.

Later on, we passed a man welding a wagon axel with a gas torch. We rode through the spray of glowing orange sparks, and I took comfort in the scene. Welding looks the same no matter where we go.

The roads were also clogged with bicycle riders carrying the few possessions they had, including farm tools and pigs. Bicycles are essentially the same all over the world.

I saw a gas generator charging hundreds of 12-volt car batteries. These batteries were the sole power source for the endless hand-built shacks we rode past.

The smell of human sewage was everywhere – after all, there was no place to go but in the swamp. Where did their drinking water come from? How did they stay healthy? Not sure we really wanted to know the answer.

Occasionally new Toyota trucks, bearing the logo of foreign Non-Governmental Agencies (NGOs), passed us. These were the same groups I had seen advertise on TV, soliciting donations to help people in impoverished countries with things like a better system of hygiene.

Soon after, we were passed by a man in a United Nations (UN) truck. His look of concern through his closed window as he saw us gave me pause. How was this country held together?

However, after several hours we grew more comfortable with our surroundings and stopped at one of the many open-air food stalls along the road. It consisted of home-made chairs on a dirt floor, covered by a dried leaf roof.

Cindie learning Khmer from kids at a food stall.

Tim (wearing mask for dust) checking out the local bike shop.

This is when we realized that the growing list of Thai words we had learned was worthless here. The people of Cambodia speak Khmer, which is unique in sound and alphabet. We did not even know the words for "hello" and "thank you." It was time to pull out our phrase book again.

Cindie peered into cooking pots searching for anything she could recognize. Many of the pots left us asking each other: "what is that?"

Cindie picked one that had rice and some kind of bean cooked with condensed milk. I was still too shocked by the desperate poverty to eat. A curious group of children had gathered around us by now, so Cindie used the opportunity to learn the local language. She pointed at words in our Southeast Asia phrase book and the kids would pronounce it for us. They thought the way I struggled to pronounce "thank you" ("ah-kun") was funny and begged me to repeat. After the initial depressing images of Cambodia it was refreshing to feel the warmth of the people.

We rode on, not stopping until our first city of Sisophon. We sought refuge in an upscale hotel suggested in our guide book as a favorite of UN employees. Upscale, in this case, cost US $6, assuming you passed on air conditioning. We had experienced enough for one day.

The next day the road grew worse. It was entirely dirt and dust. Fortunately, we had been warned of this and brought along surgical masks, which are commonly worn in cities in Asia to combat more than just the flu.

We also soon learned a bicycle's place in the road hierarchy. Trucks and buses were rare but commanded the road. Next were cars, then motor scooters and only after that the bicycle. Few people were on foot.

I was never sure where animal carts fell into this equation. They were the slowest on the road, but their power, mass and independent thinking (or at least as much as a water buffalo can think) caused others to give them lots of space.

We did not fit into the established pecking order. We were faster than all other bicycles, but slower than the motor scooters. Often, in the entire width of this dusty road, there was only one smooth track for two-wheeled transportation. The scooter operators, believing they had first dibs, routinely tried to force us to make room for them as they pulled up next to us.

The first few times they tried to force us off the track and into the dust, I was polite and slowed down to let them pass. However, this soon grew old. Every time we slowed down, with our heavy loads, we expended a lot of energy getting back up to speed.

Eventually we learned to be more aggressive, like I was in city traffic or even in a bike race. Lucky for us the scooters were underpowered and we had faster accelerations. Eventually, they got up to speed and blew past us, which solved the problem.

We made several stops that day because we could only bear so much dust and heat. We were never alone.

Despite their dark history, the Cambodians were warm

Cindie (wearing a mask for dust) on the road to Siem Reap.

and welcoming. Many spoke some English, which they had learned while attending school in refugee camps in Thailand during the Khmer Rouge era. They never spoke of the terrible past and we did not ask. Instead, they wanted to know why we came to Cambodia. How long we were staying? Where else we were going?

And by the way, they added, who were these western people they saw occasionally passing by in buses? Many Cambodians were only beginning to understand what a "tourist" was.

Amazingly, despite the increasing visits from Thailand, we were the first tourists they had actually spoken to. To them, it was a good sign – a sign that Cambodia was moving on. That's one of the benefits of cycling. The slowness of a bicycle put us in touch with the everyday people, in small villages where buses passed by in clouds of dust with passengers giving barely a glance.

And so, we drew a polite crowd in these tiny places. They studied our bicycles and our shoes. Children touched my shin or felt my hair to see if it was real. At first I feared pick-pockets—years on the road, especially in the bandit-filled regions of Latin America, have made me cautious. Unlike South America, where sneaky youths were frequently trying to put hands in my pockets or open the zippers of my packs, no one in Cambodia seemed to even think of it. Poverty does not equal crime.

At one of our many rest-stops in makeshift restaurants, the owner spoke refugee-camp English.

Locals brave the dust on their bikes too.

"You want steak?" He asked.

Cindie immediately said yes – she was craving some red meat.

Tim taking a plate of 'Snake' from a local.

Ah Yes, fried "Snake".

On the other hand, I was suspicious. No one can afford steak in this part of Cambodia, and this certainly did not look like a steak house.

"Let's get two plates," said my hungry wife, her guard down.

I asked the owner to repeat himself. Good thing: it wasn't steak he was offering. It was "snake."

Then the man presented us with a bowl of fried snakes— scales, tails, and all. Cindie, suddenly, was not so hungry after all.

We soon realized this was a lunch spot for farm hands. Most of them were skillfully using chopsticks to nibble on the small fried crawlers. No one could understand our surprise. Yes, of course it's fried snake. What's wrong with that? They had no idea we'd never seen this before.

Cindie quickly pulled our camera out. The snake salesman was happy enough to pose, but obviously could not figure out why this was a photo moment. It would be like a Cambodian tourist in the USA wanting to take a picture of a Big Mac.

He offered to take my snake order again while Cindie caught the whole hilarious moment on video. When she was filming several people crowded in wanting to be filmed as well.

Did we try it? Well, snake is a bit greasy, we reasoned, and doesn't mix well with hard cycling. We bought some warm bottles of water and passed on the reptiles until next time.

Tim in a mask, covered with dust and sweat in Kralanh, Cambodia.

By mid afternoon we reached a village with a hotel, or "guest house" as they are often called here. We could have pushed on to Siem Reap, the place where those buses filled with foreigners were headed. Instead we decided to pass on the Western amenities for one more night we wanted to stay off the beaten track once again.

It also didn't hurt that we were tired. We were both covered with a thick coat of dust. At least the fine red powder didn't invade our waterproof panniers; otherwise it would have contaminated our water filter and laptop. The clothes we were wearing were not so lucky—we threw the garments into a plastic bag. The next morning, we tied the toxic lump on the outside of my load, planning to deal with it later.

Thus free of our hardened shell of dust and sweat, we showered and put on refreshingly clean clothes from our bags. Feeling human again, we walked around the village, looking for a place to eat.

We had to choose carefully. People in the undeveloped regions of the world do not get the best cuts of meat. In fact, what would be used for hot dogs and head cheese in the United States makes up the major share of dishes here – bones, heart, lungs and intestines. To complete the meal, there's plenty of rice. And dust – always dust. The "Real Cambodia" is not without its discomforts.

The next day we battled more dust and heat until the road suddenly turned to smooth pavement. Rural Cambodia quickly disappeared and we entered the city of Siem Reap.

Truck used to haul people, animals and crops.

Locals traveling in overloaded trucks: Cambodian taxi.

Chapter 4
In the Ruins of Angkor Wat

The main temple of Angkor Wat.

The first signs of progress we passed were several ultramodern, five star hotels. Just like the Thai-filled casinos at the border, these hotels seemed to be transplanted from somewhere else—Daytona Beach, Florida or Cancun, Mexico perhaps.

Plush air-conditioned hotels are built solely for the international "haves", located just outside of these plush behemoths are homemade wooden carts pulled by teams of water buffalo with friendly, toothless drivers.

After cycling through the Siem Reap strip, we reached the

more affordable backpacker-hotel zone. That is where Cindie bargained hard for a room while I watched the bikes. We were planning to stay for a while, which is always a good bargaining tool.

This time, unlike South America, Cindie had the harder job. The hoteliers, experienced by several years of busy tourism, were hard bargainers. And for me there was nothing to watch for – no one was interested in touching our bikes. The only one to even talk to me was a man who offered me a chair from his house to sit down on while I waited. I wished I spoke more than a few words of Khmer. Instead, I had to settle for his hand gestures for "welcome" and a gentle pat on my back and hoped my smile would prove sufficient thanks.

Siem Reap (you have to say all the vowels to pronounce it correctly) is a boom-town. Even before the road was safe to travel, an airstrip was built to shuttle in tourists.

Why the hubbub? Two words: Angkor Wat.

This is, quite simply, one of the world's most majestic temple complexes. The name refers to the region's largest and most majestic temple. In fact Angkor is one of more than a dozen temples and surrounding edifices, all built by a variety of Hindu and Buddhist kings over five centuries.

Eventually, it was sacked by a neighboring kingdom, and abandoned for centuries before French archeologists began to investigate the region in the late 1800s. Thus began a process more than a century long to uncover and restore the complex.

Only a few years ago, Angkor Wat was laced with land mines and home to rogue Khmer Rouge fighters. Today, it's one of Asia's greatest destinations, and attracts up to one million visitors a year. Even grizzled backpackers, jaded after months in India or other countries filled with ruins, can't help but be captivated by the majesty of this place.

We spent a week here, and never tired of exploring these stone monuments.

The popularity of Angkor Wat has turned Siem Reap into Asia's newest boom-town. Of course, some of the backpacking tourists were appalled that Cambodia now had five-star hotels. Such class certainly takes away from the adventure of third-world travel.

That is how it is when you travel on the cheap. You always want to get somewhere before it is "spoiled." To the locals, all this success is, of course, welcome. They believe that the money coming in is the ancient kingdom's way of taking care of the people after so much tragedy.

Obviously, big hotels are quite an improvement from war or genocide. And jobs as tour guides, maids, and bellhops, while perhaps not the most glamorous professions, are considerably more appealing than forced labor and conscripted soldiering – or for that matter, working in the hot, snake-filled rice fields.

The next day, three bike tourists rolled up to our hotel, the Smiley Guest House. They were from North America – Pat, a railroad engineer from Sudbury, Ontario; Rob, a Polish-born computer programmer, formerly from Canada now living in London; and Alan, an upstate New York journalist in the midst of a six-month journey across Asia.

David from Malaysia, Tim, Alan and Cindie from USA.

The three had met on the internet and arranged to travel together through Cambodia and Laos.

They certainly had a different view of cycling than we did. For us, two was company. For them three was a party. Even though we all were about the same age I felt like the old married man, watching them go out every night to explore the burgeoning nightlife of Siem Reap.

We told the group about our Web site and book, and Pat said, "The Road that Has No End? I've seen it."

Later in the evening we went out to dinner. Just before we left, David, a cyclist from Malaysia, showed up. Pat, Rob and Alan had been emailing him. When he heard we had plans to travel through Malaysia in a year or so, he invited us to visit him.

We found a noodle stand, which had cheap plastic tables and chairs set up on a claimed section of sidewalk. Pedestrians walked through the "restaurant" as we waited for our meals.

We made a toast – "Welcome to Cambodia"—with cans of ABC Stout, a surprisingly tasty beer (most brews in Asia are sad, watery, uninspired lagers). We filled each other in on where we had been and where we were going.

Alan had spent four months in Nepal, Tibet and India. He had trekked through the Himalayas and biked through the Indian desert of Rajasthan, stopping to enjoy the world-famous camel fair of Pushkar. Then, having fallen for a Swedish woman of Indian descent, he joined her to visit Pune, the Indian city of her birth and adoption.

Pat, on the other hand, was taking his annual two-month holiday in Asia, which he does every year. Pat hates winter. So he saves all his vacation days and escapes winter to spend his time drinking and biking (in that order) through Southeast Asia. To his friends, he is known as "Siamese Pat," however after a few days here he decided to change the moniker to "Pol Pat."

Rob, the youngest of the three, had quit his computer job to pedal through Asia. He was planning on a year or more for the journey, which would take him across Southeast Asia and up through the Himalayas.

Pat, Tim, Rob and Alan at an outdoor restaurant in Siem Reap.

Three men, three different journeys. Together, the five of us made quite a team.

We spent a few hours sitting on the sidewalk of that busy street, talking about life on the road and what we hoped to get out of our respective travels.

"You know," I said to Alan at one point, "we don't usually meet many Americans when we're traveling."

"I know," he agreed. "It's sad. I heard something like only 10 to 20 percent of Americans even have passports. And most of them are going to Canada, Mexico, or maybe England or France."

"Why is that?" Rob asked.

Part of that was vacation time, we explained to the Canadians. Many Americans get only two weeks off per year, and some do not even get that (such as those working part-time jobs, or running their own small business). Because America is so isolated geographically, traveling to most foreign countries must include an expensive and long flight. And, of course, America is such a huge place that most Americans barely see much of their own country, much less other places.

That's only part of the answer, Alan added. The fact of the matter is many Americans are strangely apathetic about the outside world. Print and television journalism focuses almost entirely on domestic issues, with so much attention paid to squabbling political parties that there's little room to talk about the rest of the world.

Combine that with the fact that few Americans can speak a foreign language, and the result is; many people have no interest in going to a place where they might have trouble communicating, where everything from the food to the culture is different.

"It takes them too much out of their comfort zone," said Alan, who obviously did not have that problem. "It's a shame. Perhaps we wouldn't be so ready to start wars if we knew more about other places and cultures."

He launched into the story of how he spent eight weeks traveling in Pakistan only a few months before 9/11. When the rest of America was convinced the Muslims of the world were banding together to fuel America's destruction, Alan was remembering how he had not heard an unkind word during his entire stay, and most of the Pakistanis who talked to him about the United States had a positive view of the country.

By the time we left the outdoor "café," we had solved most of the world's problems and were ready to become tourists again.

The next day Cindie joined Alan and Rob for a pre-dawn bike ride to the Angkor Wat ruins. It's about a four-mile ride down flat roads to the gate, where you pay US $40 for a three-day ticket (the minimum you need to really appreciate the temples, although a week is better) Cindie and I had a seven-day ticket and already had spent two days exploring the ruins.

The first thing they saw was a band of tawny rhesus macaque monkeys, hanging out on the side of the road. The cyclists stopped to take pictures, and the curious, dog-sized animals began to examine the bikes. Alan thought he would chase them away. Yet, when he moved threateningly toward one of the bigger males, the male not only held his ground, he actually chased Alan back. Clearly, they were not primates to be trifled with.

The three eventually retrieved their bikes and rode to Angkor Wat, the most well known of all the temples in this complex. A crowd was already gathering for sunrise, so they locked up their bikes and walked inside.

On the way in, they were met by a group of young children selling postcards. This is a common sight at many of the temples at Angkor Wat, unfortunately, for some families this is the only way they make money.

Cindie keeping an eye on an aggressive macaque monkey.

Between the 9th and 13th centuries, a succession of Khmer kings ruled from Angkor. It was one of the mightiest and richest kingdoms of Southeast Asia, and they used their wealth to build some of the world's grandest temples. Though Cambodia is now a Buddhist kingdom, Hindus originally built Angkor and many of its subsidiaries. Its various statues and etchings reflect the gods of what was once a vast following in this country.

The largest temple in the compound, also called Angkor Wat, consists of a huge stone-wall surrounding the temple, with its almost vertical staircases and its iconic three spires. Statues of gods and goddesses adorned the walls.

Later that morning, Pat and I – preferring to sleep late – met the rest of our group and we visited more of the temples.

Temple Bayon, Buddha reaching enlightenment.

Temple Ta Prohm was taken over by the jungle.

Apsara at Ta Prohm.

From there, we rode along well-paved and flat roads to Angkor Thom, a huge stone wall with a serene Buddhist face atop the gate. There, we crossed a bridge of headless statues – the heads having been stolen by raiders many years ago.

The road led to Bayon, a massive jumble of stones and more faces. These were the faces of Avalokitesvara, a bodhisattva, or enlightened being, who is said to embody all the goodness of the Buddha himself. At Bayon, there were more than 200 of these faces, all looking faintly bemused with a vague smile and piercing stone eyes. It was hard to leave such a peaceful place.

Nonetheless there were a lot more temples to see. Over the next three days, we saw as many as possible, such as Preah Khan, the Sacred Sword, an interesting temple that has been

Land mine victims playing instruments at temple Preah Khan.

Monks at Temple Bayon.

partially rebuilt. To reach the center of the complex requires walking through one stone doorway after another. Walking down the straight hall is like walking through a hall of mirrors.

Along the path to the temple we saw a group of men, all missing limbs from land mines, playing homemade musical instruments. The music was pleasant and added to the ambiance of the temple.

One of the most popular temples here is Ta Prohm, because it was never truly restored. The jungle has encroached on this temple and the archeologists said, "Better not touch it." Today, the stone-walls are covered with massive trees with roots that ooze over and through the jumbled blocks. In some places it seems like the roots themselves are holding the temple together. In the evening, when most of the tourists have gone, it is easy to lose yourself in such a place.

The next day was Christmas Eve, though it certainly did not feel like it. The five of us originally planned to leave that morning to start our two-day ride to the Cambodian capital of Phnom Penh. However, with the previous night's activities, we decided to take a day to relax first.

It was a good thing. That morning, Alan checked his email and received a frightening message from his brother. The subject line read, "CALL AS SOON AS YOU GET THIS."

He did, and through a phone line rife with static, his mother told him, "Your father's gone."

George Wechsler, 73, was crossing a road at night several

Roots holding together the temples at Ta Prohm.

days earlier while listening to a book on tape. He was struck by a car and thrown 50 feet. Rescue workers immediately sent in a helicopter to bring him to a nearby hospital in Long Island. But the damage was such that nothing could be done. He died later that night.

It was an accident tinged with irony. When Alan had left four months earlier, his father had fretted over his journey and all the potential danger he might face across the world.

The road to Tonle Sap.

Gathering water from a well.

Yet it was his father who found harm's way, only four blocks from home, in a place he had been thousands of times before.

Alan also learned the funeral was scheduled for a day later. His family is Jewish, and Jewish funerals are always held as soon as possible after a death. Numb from shock, Alan spent several hours on the phone trying to arrange for an immediate plane back to Bangkok and then to New York's JFK Airport so he could make the funeral on time. After all that work, he finally realized that when the sun set here in Cambodia this day, his father would already be buried back home.

Alan had to settle for writing a eulogy that would be read at his dad's funeral.

Still, his family needed him, and he knew he would have to return home. It was not easy – he still had two months left in his planned trip, and he, like the rest of us, had fallen in love with Cambodia. We decided we would delay our departure so we could spend one more day together cycling through the countryside before we separated for good.

The next day we rode single-file down a road to nearby Tonle Sap, Southeast Asia's largest lake. None of us really knew what to say to him all day. He was faced with the double whammy of losing his father and his dream bike ride through Asia. We just tried to make his last day on the bike in Asia memorable.

Fishing on Tonle Sap.

Floating house on Tonle Sap.

Chapter 5
On the Road to Phnom Penh

Rob, Pat and Cindie in a pace line.

The next day, Alan headed for the airport and the four of us headed in the other direction, toward Phnom Penh, the nation's capital.

Immediately, we faced a headwind that would dog us all the way to Cambodia's biggest city. Riding into the wind is like paddling upstream or riding up a hill that never ends.

When it is just Cindie and me, a headwind means that our days are shortened.

With four of us, the riding was much easier. We could ride in a pace line. Using such a line, one rider behind the other, each close enough to "draft" off the rider in front, the wind is partially blocked and riding becomes 30 percent easier.

This technique is as old as cycling itself. Bicycle road racers always ride in big packs or lines. The one at the front of the group is not winning the race but instead just working harder. They are said to be "pulling." This is why they rotate and take turns. The top racers – the Lance Armstrongs – stay back until they are ready to attack, saving their energy for the final battle.

When it is just Cindie and me, I am usually the one in front. With the Canadians joining us, we had a total of four riders taking turns at the front of the pace line.

Not all touring cyclists know of the advantages of drafting. In fact, Pat and Rob had never tried it, and were not sure it was worth the effort at first.

Drafting is something that has to be felt instead of explained. When we left Siem Reap, Cindie took her usual position behind me and I rode behind Pat. Rob and Pat did their own thing.

Pat, riding in front, was always surprised to look back and see Cindie and me still behind him and not even out of breath. Rob, who was off to the side watching and was, in fact, out of breath, decided to move behind Cindie. He soon felt his effort reduced too.

Once Pat tired, Cindie and I showed them both how to take turns at the front. A flat road with a good headwind is the perfect teacher of drafting physics and the efficiency of riding in a group. Instead of four individuals battling the wind, we became a team and worked together.

After a few hours of efficient riding, we pulled over for lunch. Thus began an event that shall forever be known in Cambodia as "The Incident of the Chair."

This outdoor food stall had the usual assortment of cheap, flimsy plastic chairs, the sort that sell in Wal-Mart for a few bucks. You see these chairs all over Asia, and they are usually sufficient to hold my weight.

Not this time.

At this particular stop, the ground I was sitting on was not level. That meant only two of the four legs were planted on the ground. This proved too much for the plastic chair to bear.

As a crowd of Cambodian children and adults stared, the chair gave a loud "crack!" I fell to the ground in a heap. The crowd, including my Canadian buddies and my loving wife, laughed so hard they began to cry.

One of the locals, once he finally regained control, offered me another chair. By this time, most of the children had fallen all over each other, and were still on the ground, laughing away.

Once the crowd finally quieted down, I pointed at the chair and at my wallet: let me pay for the damage. The lady who was in charge, held up several fingers – enough Cambodian Riel to buy five chairs. Highway robbery for sure! However, I did not want to argue.

Children having a good laugh over the broken chair.

Still, since I now effectively owned the chair, I would take it with me. I told the lady this in English – I doubt she understood—and the group watched as I picked up the broken chair and placed it on the back of my bicycle.

Then the bike fell over.

This time, the laughter was almost spasmodic. Even people from across the street were coming by to see what all the fuss was about.

I picked my bike up and threw my arms in the air, as though I had just won a major European bike race. This was well-received, and locals gave me a round of applause.

Eventually, we all climbed back on our bikes and rode away. I know that this small Cambodian village, without even the luxury of electricity, will pass down to generations to come the story of the giant foreigner in tight clothing who broke the chair. The road may not always be a glamorous place, but it is often memorable.

On the third day out of Siem Reap, Cindie and I achieved a trip record for the most distance in one day: 134 kilometers, or about 83 miles. Our Canadian friends were in a hurry to get to Phnom Penh, with its cold beer and hot nightlife (such that it is in these parts).

With the four of us taking turns at the front of the pack, this record day was far easier than shorter days in Latin America, which usually included rough roads or huge climbs. It takes more than kilometers to make a day hard. In fact, I have a permanent scar on my right knee, from when I crashed descending a long dirt road in the Peruvian Andes, to remind me just how long days can get.

We entered Phnom Penh. In terms of city traffic, it put Bangkok to shame.

Cindie and I had thought we were worldly travelers. We thought we were seasoned to intense foreign metropolises and frenetic city life. Then we entered Phnom Penh.

We realized how wild Cambodia's capital was when we cycled into the city. Apparently this country, after years under a military dictatorship, had no more use for rules and police. There was no law enforcement, no parking rules, no stoplights, lane markings or other traffic control devices. It was Chaos Theory with combustion engines, and we were in the middle of it; trying to pedal to a hotel – at this point, any

Crazy traffic in Phnom Penh.

hotel.

At intersections, traffic slowed barely enough for individual vehicles to pick their way around each other – a game of chicken with no car insurance. Horns were applied liberally, and pedestrians took their lives in their hands.

For all this madness, we only saw one accident, which was quickly followed by a fist fight. Riding our bikes, needless to say, was a white-knuckle experience.

We eventually made our way to a backpacker hotel near the middle of town. It was sparse but a welcome respite from the crazy streets.

Once we settled in, we went to an internet café and saw pictures of what the rest of the world had seen for several days – The coast of Southeast Asia, India and more had been decimated by a massive tsunami. More than 230,000 people had died. The scope of the devastation was hard to take in. When we travel, we experience people individually or in small groups. This huge number was the population of a large city.

The moment it happened, we had already left Siem Reap, hundreds of kilometers away from the beach riding through a remote stretch of inland Cambodia on our way to Phnom Penh. In rural Cambodia, electricity is spotty and internet nonexistent. In poverty stricken areas of Cambodia literacy rates are low therefore, newspapers are rare. For several days the only way we knew about the terrible disaster was from frantic reports from the British Broadcasting Corporation (BBC) that crackled over our shortwave radio without which we would have been clueless. Even though it was on the radio it did not seem real because nobody around us knew about it or reacted to it.

The quake, which lasted 8 to 10 minutes (the longest ever recorded), caused a huge rupture in a once thought dormant plate estimated to be 1600 kilometers (approximately 1000 miles) long and 15 meters (50 feet) high in some areas. This sudden movement along the plate, caused a surge of water of an unimaginable scale to hit Bangladesh, Malaysia, Maldives, Myanmar, Thailand, Indonesia, India and Sri Lanka

It hit in classic tidal-wave fashion – and in some places the water was first sucked out to sea from the beaches. The sudden, exposed ocean floor attracted curious spectators, who

Tim, Pat and Rob in Phnom Penh.

Women selling green lotus in Phnom Penh.

were now standing on the most dangerous spot on earth. A few minutes later the ocean came back with a vengeance, not as a cresting wave but as towering swells, muscling its way kilometers inland, turning cars and rubble into deadly projectiles that destroyed anything in their path.

Though the earthquake struck hours before the tsunami, no one had warned the many villagers and city residents on the coast. There was no early-warning system, though seismologists who knew of the quake immediately must have known of the risk.

The resulting disaster affected dozens of countries around the world, as high-end seaside resorts in Thailand were as doomed as thatch villages on the poorest islands of Indonesia. Wealthy Westerners drowned as easily as their poor Asian counterparts. Rarely has a natural disaster affected such a broad spectrum of nations.

For Cindie and I, who have spent so much time in the Third World, we wondered how the locals would fare. Those foreigners who survived would be helped by their embassy, given food, money, clothes and tickets back home to recover. What of those who had no home to go back to? They will probably be living in shanty houses, solely focused on food and survival for years to come—while bureaucracy and corruption squander their intended aid resources.

We have seen this pattern before. Those already close to the survival line before the disaster will suffer the worst after, and be remembered the least.

It is a sad truth of the unequal world we live in.

Our email account was full of worried letters from our family and friends in at least 10 countries and two languages, all of whom imagined us holding onto our bikes while floating through flooded lowlands. Followers of our web site, who did not think we were dead, were now expecting us to post pictures and stories of how we survived the rushing water.

Not quite. In fact, we were far from it.

We easily could have been there. Had we decided to stick with our original plan to cycle south of Bangkok instead of east, who knows what might have happened? We personally knew of several travelers who were supposed to be in the affected areas. Were they victims? We never got replies to our emails. Even now, we have no way of knowing if they simply changed accounts, or reached their end in a wall of water.

It took a while to recover from the news of this huge disaster. Eventually, we unpacked and set out to explore this crazy city of Phnom Penh.

The first place we went to visit was the Tuol Sleng Genocidal Museum, combine that with a visit to Choeung Ek, the Killing Fields, where so many of Pol Pot's victims were buried in mass graves, and we had quite a sobering experience.

Tuol Sleng is a former prison, originally known as SP21. It was where people were tortured and interrogated by the Khmer Rouge before they were sent to the killing fields at Choeung Ek.

The grounds used to be a high school. It was left in the same condition as the Vietnamese found it in 1979, which is

Photos of prisoners at Tuol Sleng Genocide Museum.

when they pushed the Khmer Rouge out of Phnom Penh. Step through the door here, and you step back in time to Cambodia's dark, dark past.

The bottom floors, where the large cells were, are now filled with the photos of prisoners that were found there. This is the most disturbing part of the experience. Room after room of the same mug shots of those brought here for interrogation. The same pose, frontal black-and-white photo, over

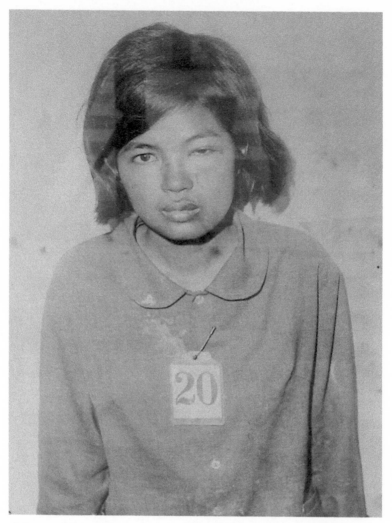

Many of the photos were just painful to look at, like this one.

and over again.

The Khmer Rouge, as bureaucratic as it was dictatorial kept records of every person that entered the prison. People of all ages, and numerous nationalities were photographed.

All were Asian save for one Australian. What was he doing there? Was he a member of the press? Or just an unfortunate visitor with exceptionally-bad timing? The prison had no information.

At first, the faces meant nothing to us. Soon we could see the emotions behind the photos—sheer fright in some of the women's eyes, the defiance in some men. Some appeared badly beaten, others already starving. Few of those in the photographs would survive their captivity. Most of those guarding them were children, age 10 to 15. They were probably scarred for life by taking part in such atrocities.

Cindie had to leave this room halfway through; she was so overwhelmed by the impact of those pictures. They will haunt both of us for a long time to come.

But we had to look. We have to remember what happen here, so it does not happen again. It is hard to imagine that people could be so pointlessly ruthless, cruel and evil to their own people. Then again, the world's history is full of such monsters. The 20th Century alone ranged from Hitler and Stalin to the modern genocides in Rwanda and Bosnia. Let us hope this new century brings better leaders.

We eventually continued to the second floor. There, the cells were much smaller, large enough only for one person. The outer balcony was covered with fencing and barbed wire so no one could commit suicide by jumping off.

Another building contained the torture devices. There was a hand-sized vice, used for the ripping off of fingernails. Alcohol was then poured on the open wounds. There was a

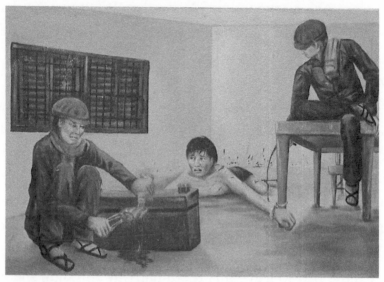

A hand-sized vice was used for ripping off fingernails. Alcohol was then poured on the open wounds to inflict pain.

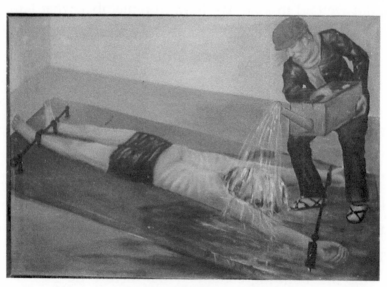

A technique used to simulate the sensation of drowning.

Another torture technique to simulate drowning.

The actual torture devices used by the Khmer Rouge.

93

tank where a person was shackled, then the tank was filled with water and the victim was forced into a near drowning experience repeatedly, similar to the torture technique called water boarding. One prisoner, who somehow survived this, painted scenes depicting the happenings inside. These paintings were hanging on the walls, leaving little to the imagination.

We also visited Choeung Ek, the killing fields. There are different reports about how many people were killed here— they range from 17,000 to 40,000. At the site there is a tower with 8,000 skulls arranged by sex and age.

Forty-three of the 129 mass graves in this area still remain undisturbed. The rest have been excavated, and visitors can walk from one pit to another. Nearby is a large tree where babies and children were beaten to death, so that bullets would not be wasted.

While walking in the hot sun, looking down at the open pits, Cindie became queasy. Looking down we could see bits of bone, teeth, and pieces of clothing coming to the surface. Our minds became numb, trying to understand why anyone would take part in such atrocities.

Fortunately, Phnom Penh had other distractions to take our minds off what we had seen in the Museums of Death.

After recovering from that visit, we visited Cambodia's National Museum. This place has relics from Angkor Wat and other archeological sites around the country. It is there that we met Seden, a Buddhist monk who helped lift us out of

Torture device above, how it was used below.

Skulls excavated from pits at the Killing Fields (Choeung Ek).

Painting depicting the killings at Choeung Ek.

The pits at the Killing Fields.

Decomposed clothing and bones at the surface.

Tim and Seden, the monk, at Cambodia's National Museum.

the funk that hit us after visiting the atrocities sites.

We had seen monks almost every day during our travels in Southeast Asia, but never spoke to them. Besides the language barrier we never knew if we were allowed to talk to them. They seemed like bald ghosts, floating around in long, flowing, orange robes.

About mid afternoon, we were walking around the hot buildings, looking for a place to sit down. A seated monk, dressed in the usual clothes, pointed to some empty chairs next to him. "Please," he said in heavily accented English. "Sit down."

Surprised to find a monk who spoke our language, we did.

"Where are you from?" He asked. We told him.

"America," he said. "You are most welcome."

His name was Seden, he said, and he was 24 years old. He liked to practice his English, and would we mind if he spoke to us? Many people in Asia do the same thing with tourists, and we are usually happy to oblige. We were especially pleased, though, to have the chance to converse with one so learned.

"I am usually in classes," he said, explaining that he attended a seminary for monks. "Today is holiday."

This day, in fact was the day in 1979 that the Vietnamese liberated Cambodia from the Khmer Rouge. A good day indeed. We were happy to celebrate with the Cambodians.

We chatted a bit, and then he said, "Please, may I show you the temples near my home?"

We left the museum and he took us to a wat (temple) near the home he shared with other monks-in-training. Seden explained the various aspects of Buddhism, although he never tried to convert us. Buddhism teaches, among other things, tolerance for other religions and ways of life – even things they do not necessarily agree with. The world would be a better place if we all took such lessons to heart.

We also found out that sticking close to a monk is the safest way to travel around this congested city. When we were

A monk in his room with his books and DVDs.

walking with Seden, his bright orange robe parted traffic better than the similarly-colored traffic cones used back home.
Drivers of cars, trucks, buses and scooters alike were respect-
ful of our space. He never even looked for oncoming cars—
just slowly walked into the thickest traffic, and the vehicles
parted around him, fearful of hitting a holy man. Moses himself could not have done any better.

The real treat was when he took us to his dorm room.
There were several monks sitting on the floor in their orange

robes, watching a Japanese movie on a desktop computer. When I asked what they were watching, one of the younger monks, who also spoke English, handed me the DVD case. It was some kind of martial arts movie dubbed in Khmer; the language of the Cambodian people.

We looked around the room and saw few possessions except an extra orange robe hanging out to dry, school supplies, and a lot of well-used books in several languages. I was surprised to see CD cases for Norton System Works™, MS Windows XP™, and MS Office™.

"Technology is like a tool," Seden said. "It is like book or pen. It can be used for good or for bad."

We sat with Seden for a long time, and asked many questions. Monks, he explained, are basically students who concentrate on religious study and meditation. They learn the teachings of Buddha and other academic subjects, especially languages.

"I am learning 12 other languages," he told us. Unfortunately, Spanish – our other language besides English – was not one of them.

He also told us that monks could not play sports or exercise, and had to follow complicated rules of diet. We were getting hungry by now, and offered to buy him something to eat. He declined.

He took us out to the street and pointed to some street kids selling fruit: "Buy from them." He showed us how to eat the fruit, which we didn't recognize. He would not take

Young monks in their room.

any. Finally, when we asked him what he would like, he said, "Coca-Cola."

Seden never asked anything specific about Americans or the USA, other than the weather. To him, countries were only geographical locations with different languages and customs. He was interested in the places we had traveled, but only in terms of religion and culture. To him, the people we met in Central and South America – who had seemed so overwhelmingly foreign to us at first – were as Western as we were.

Seden was also curious about our trip.

"Why do you choose this?" He asked, making a pedaling motion with his hands.

I described the joy and satisfaction we get from silently gliding down the road under our own power. He understood this, but he was still curious about our motive.

"What do you seek on your journey?" he asked. We tried to answer as best we could, by explaining that we are interested in learning about the world through its people and culture. He continued: "What do you avoid on your journey?" I started to answer with a short list of thieves, con artists, and biting insects, then he interrupted with: "Do you feel enlightened?"

How to answer such a question, especially to a scholar such as this. We tried to explain that we would not be near enlightenment until our trip was finished, years and years in the future. That seemed to satisfy him, at least a little bit. Clearly, he cared little about "what" and dwelled more on "why".

"It is better to travel well than to arrive," he said. "You are doing this. Your work is to discover your world and then with all your heart give yourself to it."

When we finally said our good-byes after several hours together, he left us with a statement I will never forget.

"We are not so different," he said. "We both are drawn to knowledge and understanding of the world around us. I seek enlightenment through Buddha. You seek enlightenment through meeting people of the world. I chant and meditate and you ride your bicycle. You are also on the path to enlightenment."

That one monk's approval outweighs every email we have received telling us to go home, get a real job, and save for retirement. And his final words of wisdom would follow us wherever we went: "You cannot travel the path until you have become the path itself".

We stayed a lot longer in Phnom Penh than we would have liked. The reason: the bank with which we had set up a business account back home.

This paperwork foul-up reminded us how far exotic travel has come. Only a dozen or so years ago, before email and ATM cards, traveling to places like Cambodia meant carrying all your money in cash, because travelers' checks weren't accepted and international banks didn't exist. Family members would not hear from you for weeks or months on end, because long-distance calls were too expensive and the Internet was only for computer geeks who spoke code, when it existed at all.

Most third-world countries did not have travel guides, so you had to rely on your wits and what information you could get from travelers you met who had already been there. Since there were few phrase books available and few locals spoke English, you would have to get by on sign language and smiles.

Certainly it was a far more difficult world to travel in those days than today. Difficulty breeds adventure, and adventure is what breeds memory.

Anyway, these thoughts came to mind during our bank problems. It seems the modern world was not so user-friendly after all.

It started in Thailand, several weeks earlier. There, we had called our bank, E-Trade, and converted our personal bank account into a business account. The idea was to gain immediate access to money from our burgeoning business: mainly sales of our new book and advertising on our web site.

What we did not realize – what no one at E-Trade had bothered to explain to us – was that once we switched accounts our ATM card would no longer be any good. Suddenly, we could not get our money.

While in Phnom Penh, we made several phone calls to the bank in order to get our accounts straightened out. We used our laptop, a microphone and earphones, via a Voice Internet Protocol, or VoIP, service. This made our long and frustrating international conversations at least affordable – it only cost us a few cents per minute this way, versus 50 cents at a phone booth.

After much struggling – and we were speaking the same language, mind you – it became clear that you could not use an ATM card with a business account.

Could we create another personal account, we asked, and then have you FedEx the new ATM cards to us here in Phnom Penh?

Well, yes, they said - after keeping us on hold for an hour. All we had to do was fax them some paperwork.

Well, we faxed, and faxed again and again. Every time we called the bank, we spoke to someone new, who had no idea who we were or what the problem was. Some of them clearly had no idea where Cambodia was, or if it was a country or a city in North Dakota. No one ever saw any of our faxes.

In the end, we spent more than a week trying to clear this up, and never got our ATM cards. Receiving our ATM cards would have to wait until we were in the more modern country of Vietnam. We finally left Cambodia with two days left on our 30-day visa. If it was not for an emergency stack of dollars in our bags, we would have been broke.

Sometimes America can seem like a third-world country too.

The last two days out of Cambodia were pleasant, except for a hectic ride out of Phnom Penh. We could have used a guide, like the bicycling guru who led us safely out of Bangkok a few weeks earlier.

Once outside the city, we faced a dusty day of travel to the Vietnamese border. When the international crossing appeared on the horizon, I was sorry to see it. Cambodia had touched us in ways few other countries had thus far.

Few countries had taught me so much about the meaning of life. While I traveled in Cambodia I looked deep inside myself and asked, "What would I have done if I was a Cambodian caught up in the violence of the Khmer Rouge? What would I have done if I grew up a rice-farmer in a remote, impoverished village?"

The little things in life are certainly appreciated more after they have been taken away or destroyed. The people of this fragile country showed us levels of unconditional warmth and kindness I never thought possible. We were sad to leave, but happy at least that Cambodia is finally finding its way out of the darkness.

Enjoying a game after work.

Seden and Tim.

Chapter 6
Two Wheels in Vietnam's Low Country

Tim riding along the Mekong River Delta.

Then we were in Vietnam.

The cultural change was immediate. In Cambodia, the border officials in their casual gray uniforms had offered us tea and joked around. The Vietnamese were having none of that. They were all business.

"Why do you visit Vietnam?" demanded the young man at the immigration desk. Like most Southeast Asian men we had met, he was slight. Unlike most others he was deadly serious. He had short-cropped hair, cold eyes and wore a neat, green uniform.

Cindie and I looked at each other, and our bicycles. Why

were we visiting? Wasn't it obvious?

"We are tourists," I said, smiling. "We have always wanted to visit Vietnam."

He ignored me, and turned to our passports. He looked at our photographs and then back at us. He looked through each passport, page by page, examining every visa carefully, as if our stamps from Mexico, Costa Rica, or Chile might mean a possible threat to Vietnamese security.

"You are from United States?" he asked, staring at the United States emblem on the cover of our blue passports.

Once again Cindie and I exchanged a glance that said, "Let's humor his silly questions. He's a bureaucrat."

"Yes," I said in a patient voice.

"Why you come to Vietnam?" he asked again.

After answering several variations of that question for the next few minutes, he pointed to an ancient-looking x-ray machine and indicated we should pull off the panniers from our bicycles and put them on the conveyer belt. This concerned me: I did not want their radiation-spewing antique ruining our laptop computer or digital camera.

I took out the bag containing the equipment, opened the top and took out the electronics. Then I set them on the counter in front of the unsmiling official. He pointed to the computer: "Turn on."

There were other border guards around, and they gathered to watch the x-ray monitor as our bags were cycled through the machine, one by one. Behind us, we could hear the first guard tapping on the keyboard to our laptop. When the bags came through the x-ray, we loaded them back on our bicycles.

When that task was complete, I walked back to the first official to retrieve our computer. I had visions of him paging through our many journal entries, or the thousands of digital photos we had saved, and hoped he did not accidentally delete something.

When I looked over his shoulder and saw what he was doing on the computer, I had to laugh: He was playing Solitaire.

When he realized I had caught him, he offered a sheepish grin and handed back the computer. Ah, we thought. Under all these layers of protocol was a human being after all.

From the border crossing of Tinh Bien, we headed southeast, threading the low agricultural wetlands of the Mekong Delta on a meandering route that would end in Ho Chi Minh City (Saigon), the nation's largest city.

It was a sweltering day, slamming us with heat and humidity that we had not felt since Central America years before. As usual we had to wake before dawn to start riding before the stifling temperature hit full-on. Midday riding would be impossible – all we could do was find shelter from the sun for a few hours.

Still, we rode through nondescript villages, past women working in lush paddies, wearing the traditional conical hats to ward off the sun. With all the water around us, it seemed

Woman leading a water buffalo from one rice paddy to another.

Living above the Mekong River.

Woman selling goods from a boat.

The floating market in Vietnam, capitalism at its best.

Washing dishes in the dirty water of the Mekong River.

we rode on bridges as often as dry land. Rivers were choked with boats of all sizes. This was a floating world we were riding through, where some live their lives rarely touching solid ground.

It was also a squalid place. The Mekong River begins its journey in China and winds through Laos, Cambodia, and finally in Vietnam. It fans out into a great fertile delta before emptying into the sea. This mighty and historic river is the transportation, drinking water and especially bathroom for millions living along its banks. We saw dead pigs and dogs floating just upstream from people brushing their teeth and washing dishes in water straight from the river. All of the houses had outhouses built over the water - squat toilets that splashed their business several meters down to the river's edge.

We were assaulted by more than pollution as we made our way into the delta. The history of this troubled country, and the role the United States played, weighed heavily on our minds.

Western domination of Vietnam came a century before the United States' involvement, when France created Indochina and began to exploit Vietnam's natural resources. In the 1950s, a free Vietnam was created, but with two nations – a communist north and a non-communist south. Soon after came the Domino Theory, and the influx of communist-fearing Americans, along with their allies (Australia, New Zealand, Philippines, Thailand, South Korea, and South Vietnam) to prop up a corrupt but pro-Western southern government. Then, in 1965, the war began.

The Vietnam War lasted eight years and killed approximately 57,000 Americans and millions of Vietnamese. It all but destroyed Vietnam, and came pretty close to wrecking America as well, with anti-war protests splitting the country in two. In 1975, two years after the war ended, Communists took over South Vietnam anyway, making the entire ill-conceived adventure for naught.

We were worried about how Vietnamese people might greet us, their former invaders/defenders. To our surprise, we

Tim at a war casualty memorial in South Vietnam.

found them to be most welcoming of Americans. In America, Vietnam is still a word that stings like a sore wound. In Vietnam, with its economic growth and large population of successful young entrepreneurs, the war is ancient history.

So it was ironic that the biggest argument we had about Vietnam was with a Westerner.

It happened during our first night in the country. We were sitting on a patio in our hotel, having a drink with a German man. He had long hair, a scruffy beard and round hippie-style glasses. He had already had a few, and appeared angry.

"How do you feel being American in this country?" he said, spraying saliva on the table as he emphasized the words.

"Have you seen the damage you did?"

He began to fill us with details of the war that he had learned from visiting museums in Ho Chi Minh City. The atrocities that most Americans have known for decades – the massacre of villagers, the defoliation of forests from cancer-causing Agent Orange, the burning of children using Napalm. None of this was our (personal) doing, so we ignored his rant.

After a while, I decided to go to bed. I hoped Cindie would follow me, but she wanted to finish her beer.

Later, Cindie told me the man doubled his vitriol after I left:

"You Americans," the man said. "Who the hell do you think you are, coming into a beautiful place like this and destroying it? You ruin everything you touch."

"Well, I didn't drop any bombs on people," Cindie said in a perfectly casual tone. "I think war is wrong."

She might have not have said a word. "Americans love to kill people," he said. "That's all you know how to do."

"Well, I've never killed anyone. No one I know has ever killed a person."

"America should use its power for good. Why do you not do that? Why?"

"America does some good," said Cindie, beginning to realize she was fighting a losing battle. "Sure we could do more – a lot more – but we're not evil."

"Americans!" he said. "I hate 'em. I hate 'em."

That was enough for Cindie. Who was this drunken buffoon to tell us how war-mongering Americans were? And a German too – there were a couple of wars last century that they had something to do with.

As Cindie walked past the hotel manager, who was standing behind a desk, the lady reached out and gently placed her hand on Cindie's arm. She had heard the argument through an open window.

"Do not worry about him," she said in English. "Vietnamese people forgive you."

Cindie felt humbled as she made her way back to her room, receiving such kind words from a stranger. Still, that night she dreamed about war, death and destruction, and woke with a huge feeling of guilt.

They were feelings that would only be shaken by experiencing the Vietnam of today.

The next day we rode to Long Xuyen (pronounced "soo in"), a nondescript mid-size city. After we found a hotel, we went out looking for a place to eat. We came across a flashy restaurant/bar and walked inside. We sat down and the next thing we knew the owner came over to join us. He was quite young, wearing stylish clothes and a trendy-looking haircut.

"This is my new restaurant," he said. "You like?"

We did, and told him.

"I am university student. I study biotechnology and English." He began to tell us about Vietnamese food, and taught us a few words in his language. Cindie wrote them down, so we could practice later.

City of Mytho, Vietnam.

Then my wife put down her pen. Her memory from last night was still fresh in her mind. "What do Vietnamese think of the war?" she asked. "And Americans?"

"War is no problem," he said. "American no problem. That

Typical lunch, pork with rice and spinach soup, with our books.

is the past. Vietnamese peoples look to the future."

Besides, he added, many families in Vietnam have relatives who have moved to the United States. "Do you know South Carolina?" he said. "I have aunt there."

Dinner was delicious. Vietnamese food is somewhat similar to Chinese, in that it is eaten with chopsticks and cooked in a wok. While the Chinese rely on sauces, the Vietnamese use delicious spices like lemon grass, keeping the final product lighter and the flavor more subtle. When dinner was over, our new friend brought us a plate of grapefruit, custard (sweet) apple, papaya, pineapple and watermelon. It seemed we were forgiven after all for having been born American.

Unfortunately, not every Vietnamese business owner was so forthright. At another town, Long Vinh, we found a hotel. As per our usual regimen, I watched the bikes while Cindie went inside to book a room.

There was no one at the desk, and as she waited Cindie saw a sign saying that rooms were 120,000 Vietnamese dong, or about US $8. When the clerk arrived and saw a Westerner in her lobby, she immediately turned the sign around. Suddenly it said US $16.

"I don't want to pay US $16" Cindie said. "I want to pay 120,000 dong."

"You are foreigner," the owner said. "You pay foreigner price." We had no choice but to pay the higher price for the room.

We soon found many of the hotels would do that, along with restaurants and other businesses. Ripping off Westerners seems to be a popular sport in Vietnam, and we would have to constantly be on alert to prevent being overcharged.

At least we were eating well. We found a restaurant next door and ordered pho, a delicious Vietnamese noodle soup with wontons, beef and vegetables.

From there we cycled a casual circle around the delta, riding past floating houses, schools, and open-air markets. One day, we hired a boat and a weathered, old woman navigated us through a maze of congested waterways and canals that connect the many arms of the delta. She used a gas motor

Living on the water.

for long distances, but would turn it off and row us through narrow areas, such as floating markets or residential areas of tightly-packed houses on stilts.

Most of the boats we saw were old and patched together. They did not look like they could float, despite evidence to the contrary. We enjoyed these motor-less moments the most. At the slow pace we could see into the market boats and watch money and goods being exchanged at a frantic pace. It looked like the trading floor of Wall Street, only cabbage and bananas were traded at market value. This was capitalism in its purest form, unhampered by government, taxes, or even communism.

We enjoyed riding through the delta, despite the heat. There were no hills to worry about, and mostly quiet villages with friendly residents. Then it was time to enter Ho Chi Minh City.

The problems began more than 50 kilometers (30 miles) outside of town. The rural landscape had already begun to morph into the outskirts of a city, with small factories, warehouses and fences of corrugated metal topped with barbed wire hiding its industrial contents from passers-by.

And traffic. Which quickly got worse and worse.

We were on an arterial road, one that on a map appeared to lead right to downtown. Unfortunately, it appeared it was also leading every motorbike, truck, bus, minivan, taxi and private car in Vietnam in the same direction. The pollution was so bad Cindie wore a mask over her mouth and nose; although I'm not sure it offered much protection against carbon monoxide and other toxic fumes.

As we moved further into the city, the traffic became thick, motorbikes filling any gaps left between cars. There was as much lateral movement as forward, as everyone pushed to compete for the limited space. This was no place for a bicycle, and yet we had no choice but to continue.

We tried to stay to the side, near the curb, but motorbikes would invariably pass us to the right and push us further into traffic. In the center of the road, there was no set median – just an imaginary line that daring drivers crossed whenever they wanted to pass. Occasional construction spots narrowed the road even further, adding to the chaos.

A din of honking and unmuffled motors made it impos-

Tim showing a map of our route on the ferry.

sible for us to hear each other, even from a few feet away, and the air was black and bitter from unfiltered exhaust. Trying to stay alive we followed the traffic over larger and larger bridges, the city increasing in size with each mile. It was the worst bike ride of our lives.

We quickly learned the nature of Vietnamese driving: survival of the fittest, with every vehicle for itself. Riding in Phnom Penh was bad, but this was something we had never experienced before. Not only did drivers have no respect for those around them, they actually seemed to want bad things to happen. It was as if the Vietnam War had been condensed to four lanes of pavement, and we were the only ones not wearing an armored vest.

The biggest problems were the motorcycles. There were two kinds: 50 cc or 110 cc (which denotes engine size and is written on the side of the gas tank). The 50 ccs were slow and easy to pass, but the larger cycles would dart in and out, and threatened to come between Cindie and me. The bikes drove so close to us we were worried their hot tailpipes might melt our panniers.

Using hand signals behind my back, I told Cindie to stay as close behind me as possible; inches from my back wheel. We had been riding together long enough that she trusted me completely and knew exactly what I was doing.

However, the motorcycle riders gave us no mercy. Clearly Vietnamese driving had become some kind of dangerous game, where men were desperate to prove their Asian *machismo*. And people did get hurt – we passed several accidents, and heard their victims screaming in pain. Neither of us could take our focus away from the road to look at what happened.

Unable to talk to Cindie amid all the noise, I worried how she was doing. I need not have bothered. While my wife has the special ability to freak out over small problems, she is also able to pull herself together in extreme situations. She cannot watch a scary movie without making sounds of distress, but on this road from hell she focused on my back wheel and kept on pedaling.

I in turn sought my inner fury that seldom comes to the surface. I powered ahead, forcing my hundred-pound loaded bike into any space I could find. At points, I would actually reach out and shove lighter-weight scooters out of my way. I was terrified, but tried not to show it.

At one point, I noticed a bus in front of us, with the heads of passengers leaning out the window looking back. It seems they were interested in seeing if we would survive. At that point, a mass of motorbikes began pushing us into the center of the road. All of a sudden, we found ourselves facing on-coming traffic.

A cyclo - a three-wheeled motorbike with a large cargo basket in front of the driver – was heading right toward us in the opposite direction. The cyclo was filled with three large pigs heading to market. The driver was lighting a cigarette and was not even looking in our direction.

Killed by pigs in Vietnam. What an inglorious way to go. I had to think fast.

I made a hand-motion to the man on a shiny Suzuki motorcycle next to me – *can we move over?* – he laughed in my face. Behind him was another man on a smaller bike. We made eye contact, and he shook his head gravely. Did he not realize that if we hit the pigs he would go down too?

They were also aware of the spectators on the bus. No one wanted to appear weak.

Survival instincts took over.

Cindie and I have developed a precise set of hand singles to communicate our moves as a unit on our loaded bikes. I patted my rear hard three times. This told her to sit tight and be ready for rapid movements.

The pigs loomed closer.

I sprinted forward and in front of the Suzuki. The driver, predictably, sped up to defend his space.

This was my bluff. When the Suzuki sped up, I filled the space behind him. Now there was enough space for me to move over.

But what about Cindie? The pig cart was almost upon us, and the man on the Suzuki had figured out my strategy. He slowed down to match me, smiling at his victory and cutting off any space for my wife.

Finally, as we moved forward at top pedaling speed, I reached out my hand to push his motorbike away with everything I had. He pushed back. The crowd on the bus went wild, cheering through the windows.

The two of us leaned into each other hard, but eventually he started to ease right. That created enough space for Cindie and me to move over. The pig cart passed me on my left, so closely I was slapped on my leg by a pig's ear. Whew!

Once we realized we were not going to die, we fought our way over to the sidewalk to take a break in front of a store that sold farming hand tools. "Thank goodness," was all Cindie said.

It took us two hours of heart-pounding cycling before we finally reached the center of the city and found a hotel. We would be pedestrians for the remainder of our stay in this city.

Vietnamese cycle rickshaw in Saigon.

Chapter 7
Americans in Saigon

Cobras in a whiskey jar, believed to be a Vietnamese aphrodisiac.

Ho Chi Minh City is what the communists renamed Saigon after South Vietnam fell in 1975. Today, it is a vast, throbbing city of 10 million people, teeming with a pulse you can only find in an emerging economy.

Aside from the climate, it is not the warmest city in the world. "It is big, noisy and polluted. At our hotel, the proprietor took away our passports and insisted that we could not leave our bikes in our room. We locked them in a back alley and hoped for the best.

Once we recovered from our morning cycle through

Helicopter at the War Remnants Museum.

Tank at the War Remnants Museum.

chaos, we went out to explore the city. Our first stop was the War Remnants Museum. We arrived around 1:30 p.m. and the place was packed with primary school children.

The museum was overwhelming too. In the first room was a diorama showing all the countries that had been opposed to the war. There were also pictures of the demonstrations that were held in the United States during that time.

From there, we moved to the torture exhibits. There was a mock-up of a prison room called a Tiger Cage, which was supposedly used by either South Vietnamese or American soldiers to interrogate Viet Cong (VC) soldiers. It reminded me of S-21 - the interrogation prison run by Pol Pot turned genocidal museum in Phnom Penh.

The most disturbing exhibit illustrated the effects of Agent Orange, the defoliant used by Americans to clear away Vietnam's lush greenery to prevent the VC from hiding. Even today, decades after the war, children are being born with no limbs, curved backs or other disfigurements due to the dioxin in Agent Orange. There were also deformed fetuses in a jar. Cindie was moved to tears.

Other exhibits included military equipment like rifles, guns, seismic bombs, and aircraft – even a helicopter. They also had an exhibit on cigarette lighters and the mottos etched into the metal (you can buy a lot of "authentic" GI lighters in tourist markets, most of them were made years after the war). There was also a pile of American dog tags. It made me wonder what had happened to the owners – I did not imagine it was good.

Children on a field trip to the War Remnants Museum.

Fetuses deformed by Agent Orange saved in jars.

The last exhibit, and we felt the best, was dedicated to journalists and photographers who died covering the war. Risky business, for sure. I recognized a number of photos that I remember seeing in magazines during my youth.

We spent about four hours at the museum and we were mentally exhausted and depressed by the time we left. It certainly was a humbling experience, and certainly made our dangerous bike journey seem like nothing compared to the horrors that had occurred here years earlier.

As I felt more confident about our presence here, I began to talk to English-speaking locals about the war and the government today. It seemed there are two different ways of looking at the end of the war and life in Vietnam today.

For instance, people who were supportive of the North during the war see the South as liberated and reunited with their northern comrades. People who preferred the Southern Government, on the other hand, see the North as violent occupiers.

Northern supporters, who saw America as imperialist invaders that had to be driven out, greatly respected America as their most fierce opponent. They were also quick to point out that the war was unpopular in the USA and knew the history of social protest against the war in Vietnam by Americans.

Southern supporters, on the other hand, had mixed feelings. While polite, they were sure to point out that America promised to fight by their side – then promptly abandoned them in 1973 to suffer the retribution of the North.

*Our guide explains that most American soldiers could not fit down
this entrance into the Cu Chi tunnels.*

After we had explored the city for a few days we signed up for a day-trip to the Cu Chi Tunnels, located just outside the city. The traffic was as brutal as ever, we were glad to be witnessing it from the relative safety of a minibus instead of on our saddles. We had already decided we would not be biking out of Ho Chi Minh City when our stay here was over, but would take a bus instead.

To understand the intensity of the Vietnamese resolve during the war, one need only visit this site. Any soldiers during wartime who spent time trying to crack these miles of subterranean tunnels must have known in his heart, an enemy who could live like this would never be defeated.

The tunnels were first built in the 1940s to hide weapons from the French-backed government. When hostilities between north and south increased in the 1960s and the United States stepped in, the tunnels were vastly increased. The region's red clay made it the perfect soil to hold the tunnels together, but that was the only easy thing about it.

The tunnels themselves were barely wide enough for a Vietnamese person to crawl through, and often too small for most Americans. Tunnels led to chambers where VCs ate, lived, used the bathroom and even underwent surgery. Temperatures were stifling – in the afternoon during the hot season soldiers had to lie on the ground in order to get enough oxygen to breathe.

The tunnels were also visited by snakes, rats, fire ants, centipedes, bats and scorpions. And it was so dark long-time residents were often temporarily blinded upon their return to the surface.

However the tunnels worked. Americans were never able to discover all of them, and were often too physically large – and too terrified – to go down in them if they did. Tunnels were booby-trapped with sharpened stakes, small bombs or boxes of snakes or scorpions set to fall on invaders when they crawled past. Even vent holes were carefully hidden inside termite mounds or surrounded with hot pepper powder so sniffing dogs couldn't find them.

Using the tunnels as a base, the VCs were able to harass the enemy for years. The tunnels played a huge role in the Tet Offensive, considered the turning point of the war.

Americans finally resorted to carpet-bombing the area in an effort to destroy the tunnels. Although by then the damage by the VCs had been done. After we arrived at the tunnels, our tour started with a movie that our guidebook warned would be inaudible. It was.

Still, watching the movie was fascinating, because it was obviously pro-North. A map on the wall near the movie screen showed how close North and South forces had been in this area. I never realized how scattered things were. I thought it was more of a battle front rather than small pockets of occupied territory. It must have been just crazy figuring out where one side's territory ended and another started.

Our guide spoke very good English and he belted out the information like he was still in the army. He showed us a very small opening that led into the tunnels that were actually three levels. The upper tier was for fighting, making

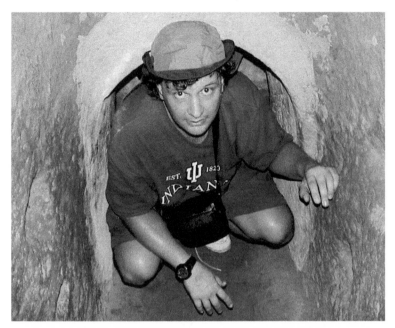

Tim squeezing through the Cu Chi Tunnels.

Replica of a pit trap hidden in the jungle to maim soldiers.

weapons, and cooking, the second and third tier were for living. They paraded us past the different traps they made to maim soldiers.

To make things all the more real, everyone on the tour could go to a shooting range and shoot an M-16 at the cost of US $1 per bullet. A lot of tourists wanted to shoot these weapons. As we walked through the jungle – now completely recovered from the decimating bombing - we could hear shots going off and at times in quick succession.

There was also an abandoned tank to visit, which had been blown up by a homemade bomb. We could still see the shrapnel indentations in the armor - whoever was in that tank did not make it back home.

It was interesting to get the Vietnamese take on the war's conclusion. Growing up in America, studying history in public schools, and watching television, it was never clear to me exactly how the war came to an end. I tried to remember what I was taught about the Vietnam War but it seemed fuzzy; possibly a tie.

The Vietnamese, on the other hand, were quite clear. They won, the USA lost. End of story.

Not only did the USA lose, we lost using some pretty underhanded tactics – other things that schools do not teach. Such as the Agent Orange that was sprayed on civilians, which was as much a chemical weapon as a defoliant. Millions of gallons were sprayed on up to 20 percent of South Vietnam's jungle in order to remove cover for the enemy.

Shrapnel holes in a blown up American tank.

Tim going into an enlarged entrance to the Cu Chi tunnels.

According to the post-war Vietnamese government (granted, not the most unbiased source), 4.8 million Vietnamese people were exposed to Agent Orange, resulting in 400,000 deaths and disabilities, and 500,000 children born with birth defects. A number of American soldiers were also affected by Agent Orange, and their children have since experienced problems as well.

It's hard to be proud of America's so-called high moral ground after riding through village after village with deformed and crippled children due to their parents' exposure to something paid for by American taxpayers.

Once again, we went home exhausted and humbled.

When we were finished in Ho Chi Minh City, we put our bikes on a bus and headed north out of the city toward the Central Highlands. It was a long ride, and extremely rough. A little girl near us was getting sick; I was not feeling much better. I get motion-sick quite easily - even on car rides in America, which seemed like a carousel compared to this roller-coaster ride. Cindie kept plying me with ginger pills, which kept my stomach settled as we lurched in and out of potholes and back and forth as we passed slower vehicles or stopped suddenly.

My gurgling stomach did not get much sympathy from Cindie after we stopped for a toilet break. The men all ran outside and peed wherever they wanted to. With no facilities anywhere nearby, the women stayed on the bus holding it in. It took seven hours to reach Da Lat, the capital of the highlands area, and Cindie had no relief until then.

140

Celebrating Tet with local coffee growers.

After the scorching heat of the delta, it was a relief to be here. The hills top out around 1,372 meters (4,500 feet) high, with pine trees, summer homes for the Saigon elite and clean air.

We spent five days there, and left Da Lat with the approach of Tet, the Vietnamese New Year. This is a week-long party involving firecrackers, flowers, and plenty of food. Houses are cleaned and decorated with yellow blossoms. The wealth of the first person through the door of the New Year reflects the family's luck for the year to come, so the rich - or in our case, foreigners - are invited to enter homes.

We were soon well out of the tourist regions, and were riding through smaller and smaller towns. At one point, we

Cindie shaking hands with the father in his kitchen/noodle restaurant.

Cindie receiving a gift of food wrapped in a banana leaf.

faced a long climb over a mountain pass, and our first night camping in Asia.

On the climb we stopped in a small village noodle restaurant and ate an early lunch. The "restaurant" was really the kitchen table of a family's house. With the tropical sun pounding down, even at this altitude, it was hot. We drank every bottle of 20-cent carbonated water they had. No one spoke English beyond "hello" and "What you name?"

As we ate, they asked, through rudimentary sign motions, if we had children or family with whom to spend Tet. "No," we signed.

To a small village family, this was a tragedy. And one they could soon rectify.

The father and obvious head of the family barked out orders in rapid-fire Vietnamese to several members of the family and they set about unknown tasks. Once everyone had returned, a large group of extended family gathered around us.

The father was a smart man. He drew his family tree on a piece of paper with stick figures. It was important to him that we understood who was who. Triangle skirts represented women and straight lines for men.

We learned the Father had three sons present. His two daughters were at their new families in a nearby village, but would visit during Tet. He gave us everyone's name – I was glad there would not be a quiz later. The three brothers patted me on the shoulder, then pointing at their family stick

143

figures to introduce the actual members.

There were babies present too, who apparently had never seen white people before. They cried at first sight, even with my best attempts to be funny.

This father was not an old man, so I asked him about his own parents by drawing stick figures above him. He responded by writing numbers on the paper and then acting out acts of violence. His father was killed in 1968 while serving in the South Vietnamese Army. His mother and several more members of his family were killed when their village was bombed, napalmed, and burned to the ground by American aircraft.

I wrote down the year of my birth – 1966 – to show I was too young to be in the war.

Don't worry, he signed, seeming to imply, I do not blame you for the war.

When we were done eating our noodle-and-pork soup, father broke into a long speech. I have no idea what he said, but it was sincere. I guessed that he officially welcomed us into his home during the Tet holiday, and wished we could be with our family during this special time. One of the young girls knew a few more words of English, and kept repeating "luck-lucky" and "Happy New Year" over and over.

As we were leaving the father gave us yet another gift – rice filled with sweet potato and peanuts, wrapped in a banana leaf, about the size of a large cucumber. I put the gift into my pannier for later, we filled our water bottles and we started up the hill.

It was 130 kilometers (80 miles) from Duc Trong to Jun Village, with no hotel along the way. We camped at a spot in the jungle where it had been cleared to put in power lines. It was not a large area but it was hidden and would do.

It was nice to see the stars; I missed camping, like we did so often in South America. The night was quiet, and we slept soundly and undisturbed.

Our camp at the top of a pass between Da Lat and the Jun Village.

Cindie waving to locals on a tractor.

Tim riding with water buffaloes.

Chapter 8
The Nasty Side of Vietnam

A long house in the Jun Village.

The next day we rode to the Jun Village, a traditional village occupied by the M'nong, one of Vietnam's hill tribes. Here, everyone lives in a long house on stilts - one big room up off the ground.

The steps up to the house were interesting – a lengthwise log, with notches cut into it to form a narrow stairway. It was entertaining to watch the dogs balance up and down the beam. We arrived in late afternoon and barely had time to

Children playing on the stairs of the long house.

take a primitive shower – a bucket of cold water in a concrete hut - before the sun went down.

Jun is a working community. Here villagers use elephants to harvest trees. It was a beautiful location next to a scenic lake, and filled with friendly villagers.

Unfortunately, we could not relax. We were sharing the longhouse with the only other foreigner, an American, Mary Ann, who was on a motorcycle tour with a Vietnamese guide. Mary Ann was nice enough, but we did not trust the guide at all.

Tim trying to keep an elephant from going through our bags.

He never gave us his name. Instead, he started asking us questions about where we had been. All of a sudden, he asked: "Do you have laptop computer?"

When we were by ourselves, I told Cindie: "I don't trust this guy." Clearly, he is interested in our stuff.

It was not a good town to be stuck with an untrustworthy roommate. The long houses had no privacy, no lockers and no locks. There was no way to keep our stuff safe. So one of us stayed by the bags at all times, while the other ate, visited the sites or even when we brushed our teeth. It was not an

149

Cindie in front of the long house adjusting the straps on her bag.

Tim with his new friend, the elephant.

Indigenous women carry their harvest from the field.

Girl waiting for her laundry to dry.

enjoyable visit.

It turns out we had reason to be cautious. When we left, Mary Ann was arguing with her guide: it seems he had doubled his price.

The next day we rode to Buon Ma Thuot, along the way we had a violent encounter with a local.

We had pulled over at one of the few open places to eat. It was only a small store with snacks, anything will do when choices are limited. The sitting area had miniature chairs and tables that always make us think of kindergarten. Cindie went looking for sandwiches and I watched our bikes.

Then a drunken man started to fiddle with our bikes. Asians have a different definition of personal space than we do, so I tried to ignore his innocent brake-handle squeezing and tire thumping.

Suddenly, he straddled Cindie's bike and wanted to ride it away.

I jumped up and grabbed him by the back of his shirt, pulling him back. He refused to get off. So I pushed him.

Like a defiant child he started pushing buttons on the bike computer. So I grabbed his hand and pulled him away. He eventually staggered off.

When Cindie returned I told her what had happened. "Be on full alert," I said.

Cindie bought a bottle of purified water from an old lady. That's when the drunken man returned. Now he was interested in the wallet that Cindie kept clenched in her hand.

He reached for it. "No!" Cindie yelled. He reached again. I stood up.

"Just ignore him," she said to me. "He'll go away."

But he did not. He kept reaching for it, perhaps playfully at first then with an increasing force. Cindie kept pushing his hands away. My blood boiled.

Finally he went too far with his tugging. Cindie angrily faced him, pointed her finger in his face, (a great insult in Asian culture) and told him "No! Don't touch my wallet!"

In these small villages, Asian men look at women as second-class citizens. Cindie's yelling and pointing was unheard of. He was about to retaliate when I stood up. For once I was glad to be a large Westerner in a country of diminutive men.

At this point, I noticed he was looking at several friends, who had pulled up on motorbikes. They were laughing – fortunately, at him, not us. The drunk was strangely quiet.

"Tim," Cindie said. "Sit down."

At that moment, the drunken man moved forward again – he was clearly upset to be humiliated before his buddies. The next thing I knew, Cindie had jumped up and grabbed my drinking water and threw it on him.

"He just hit me on the shoulder!" she shouted, turning red. "Get him away from me!"

I grabbed the drunk by the shoulders with both hands. He did the same to me. I was glad, actually - that way I knew where his hands were. When trouble is coming it always starts with the hands.

Time froze. I considered my options. I had a small, folding knife in my pocket and a small can of pepper spray. Now that we were out of South America, I had thought we would not need them, but I had them anyway. Now I weighed whether to grab one and which.

The drunk tried to push me over. No chance – I was twice his size. His eyes flashed in anger. I believe he would have killed me if he had the opportunity.

Should I grab the knife? I was just about mad enough to do it. Fortunately, logic prevailed - we did not want problems later with the police.

What about the pepper-spray? That would stop him all right. He would probably think he was blinded forever. And then what would his friends do?

Going through all of these scenarios instantaneously made me realize just how far from home we were. We were truly on our own.

The drunk still had his hands on me. Now he started to choke me. I shoved him hard into a wall. His head cracked against the stone, and he fell to the ground in a heap. Down, but not out.

He stood up again, staggering toward me. At this point all I wanted to do was leave, but he didn't know when to stop. So I ran at him, fists raised.

This time, he turned and ran. I turned to his friends and said, "I am going to kill him if you do not take him home."

No one knew what I was saying, but they understood.

They all backed away.

Cindie yelled, "Time to go, Tim!"

She tucked her half-eaten sandwich in her rear jersey pocket and climbed on her bike. The drunken man reappeared, keeping his distance while his friends kept watch.

"You go first," I told Cindie.

The drunk started to follow her and I cut him off. He stayed out of my reach, glaring. I stared him down, heart pumping furiously, until Cindie was out of range. Then I got on my own bike and rode the hell out of Dodge.

We cycled hard for a half-hour before my heart returned to its rightful place in my chest and my blood cooled. Finally, when we felt far enough away to be safe, we pulled over to debrief.

"I could have killed him!" I said.

"I know."

"I almost pulled out my knife."

"That's why I wanted us to leave so quickly," she said. "I didn't want that to happen."

"I'm glad."

We embraced, both glad the nightmare was over.

"What's wrong with some people?" I asked.

"They're human," she said.

That seemed as good an answer as any. We got back on our bikes and kept riding.

Later that day, we rolled into the medium-size city of Buon Ma Thuot, and were greeted by an old military tank, right in

Large billboard seen from the road on the way into Buon Ma Thuot.

the middle of the road. It was a monument to the Viet Cong's defeat of Americans in this city. We found a room to retreat to and collect ourselves.

I did not sleep well that night. I was still shaken up by the fight with the drunken man. Travel long enough, and you're sure to come across the wrong element at the wrong time. We had in the past and surely will again in the future. Still that did not make it any easier.

We originally planned to spend two nights in the provincial city of Buon Ma Thuot, and take in the Tet climax as the only foreigners in town. I turned on our computer and was amazed to see we had a wireless connection - the first time ever we had picked up Wi-Fi on the road from an unknown source. Another reason to stay put for a while.

Cindie is very good at managing our money - no easy task, considering how rarely we have an Internet connection. Now we had privacy, so during our first morning in town Cindie made a complete assessment of our online bank accounts and the cash we were carrying. She spent the entire morning surfing, entering passwords, and counting dollars, American Express travelers checks, and Vietnamese Dong.

When she was done, we went to lunch. On our way out the door, we told the hotel manager not to clean our room. That's our policy in every country. I often tell Cindie: "I'm not racist - I don't trust *anybody*".

When we got back an hour later, we discovered the room had been cleaned anyway. We were immediately suspicious. Cindie had left most of our money in the bags, and quickly counted.

"Tim, we've been robbed!" she said.

Her quick inventory discovered that we were down US $100 in travelers checks, US $150 in three US $50 bills and about US $66 worth of Vietnamese dong.

Our room had been cleaned out all right.

We dashed down to the manager's desk, demanding our money. One would expect a dutiful manager to call in the housekeeper and seriously question her.

Instead it was we who were interrogated by the manager, who spoke only limited English. "You sure you lose money?"

she demanded in broken English. "How you know?"

The manager called in the cleaning person. I turned to Cindie and whispered: "The manager is in on it." To the manager I said, "I want the police."

The woman suddenly looked afraid. "Police no needed," she said.

"Yes, they are."

We walked to the police station, the manager following us and protesting. When we got to the station we found it empty. The manager said, "I get police," and left.

When she came back with two police officers, we returned to our room. However, it was a dubious venture. The police, who smelled strongly of rice wine, spoke no English. So the manager – and the likely perpetrator – also had to be our translator.

As the three of them spoke rapidly in Vietnamese, I began to realize they were trying to make a deal. If the police took the woman's side, she'd cut them in on the take. Of course, Cindie and I could not talk to each other in English without the woman listening to what we said.

Fortunately, we had a secret weapon.

"She's trying to make a deal with the cops," I told Cindie in Spanish.

"What should we do?"

"I'll try to think of something we can do to our advantage."

The manager looked worried when we started to speak

158

in a language she couldn't understand. The police were concerned too. I think the manager was trying to hide the fact that she could no longer understand us.

"I bet the manager lied about how much money she stole from us," I told Cindie in Spanish. "That way she won't have to give them that much of a cut."

To test this theory, I wrote down the amount that was stolen and showed it to the cops. The manager tried to distract me.

I was right. Once I showed the police how much was stolen – remember that Vietnamese use the same numbers we do – the police grew angry. A violent barrage of Vietnamese was delivered. I could tell the manager was renegotiating everyone's cut.

"I have an idea," I said to Cindie. I walked over to our video camera and acted like it had been on the whole time and I was changing the tape. In actuality I was putting in a new tape and turning it on, but they didn't know that. I made sure they saw the red recording light as I repositioned it to take in the room.

The cops turned to me and pointed at the tape in my hand and then at his watch. How long have you been recording? The manager translated.

"Since you arrived," I lied.

The cop's facial expressions turn to fear. What would happen if their bosses saw this? The police stormed out of the room in anger, shouting at the manager. I do not know what they said, but she was practically in tears. Finally, she too left us alone.

"Tim, you're amazing," Cindie said. "How'd you think of that?"

I shrugged, smiling modestly. "I did that to my students all the time. If you make them think you can prove they're guilty, then give them a less painful way to resolve the situation, they'll take it."

"Smart," she said. "But how are they going to resolve this?"

"I don't know."

Eventually, the police came back and made us sign a report in Vietnamese. I had no idea what it said, I signed it anyway. We did not even get a copy.

Using our wireless connection and our VoIP technology, we used our laptop to call the American Embassy – which was closed for Tet. Then we called American Express in the USA. The connection was crystal-clear, and they immediately cancelled the checks and sent replacements to my parents in Indiana. Fortunately there was an ATM in town, so we could replenish our supply of cash.

The whole incident depressed both of us. Our space and trust was violated, and bad experiences in this country were starting to pile up.

Later in the day, four more men who had been sent by American Express showed up with a translator. We again told our story. We wrote down our story in English. An hour later, an immigration officer and two more cops came by. Cindie told them the exact amount that was missing and the serial numbers on the travelers checks. They said they would talk to the staff.

By now it was 10 p.m. and we were both exhausted. Cindie was not optimistic about finding our money. On the other hand, I thought we would have a chance – *someone* had our cash.

When we woke up the next morning we had a surprise: our money had been returned!

It had been slipped under the door. Everything was there except about US $33 worth of Vietnamese dong. We were shocked, but in a good way. Someone evidently thought the money came at too high a price.

At 10 a.m., no less than ten police showed up. This time we told them the good news. They took photos, measured the doorway, checked out the balcony and filled out more paperwork. They asked us if we were happy that the money was returned.

"Very much," Cindie said.

Eventually, the police told us that we would not have to pay the hotel for the room unless the bill came to more than the amount of money that was not returned.

The hotel owner was not very happy, though. She gave us a hard time when we left, demanding money for the room. We got the police again, and they let us go – after the hotel owner demanded our address and phone number. Tim made

Tim showing local boys where we are on the map.

something up and we were ready to go.

"Where you go now?" the proprietor asked us.

"Nha Trang," said Tim. It was the opposite direction from where we were headed. We did not want her driving down the road after us, cornering us in some quiet section of road with a few of her friends.

It was a relief to get out of town. We both hoped that the rest of our trip would be devoid of nasty people.

As we kept traveling, we continued to experience both the good and bad of Vietnam's two week long Tet holiday, all

One of our campsites in the Vietnam's Highlands.

around us. It made eating difficult, as roadside stands were all closed. Roads were crowded with bikes and motorcycles, and people would often slow down to ask us where we were from. Many invited us to join them in their homes.

For lunch one day, we stopped in an internet café in a nondescript town to check in with the rest of the world. The owner offered us some homemade rice wine. We declined – getting drunk would make it tough to ride.

Then he offered us "winter melon" tea. We do not know what it was exactly, but it was delicious.

We were back on the bikes in the afternoon, stomachs full of sloshing liquid. The air was cool and smelled of pines. We camped one night in a forest, quite illegally. The next morning a Western bike tourist group passed us in the opposite direction. They offered greetings as they rode by. It was easy to feel like we had left our troubles behind.

However, that did not last long. We were plugging along one day when all of a sudden I heard Cindie, riding behind me, scream in pain.

I turned my neck and could see she had not crashed, but was red in the face and crying.

"I just got hit by a rock!" she cried.

A minivan had just passed us, and that was where it must have come from. There was a man hanging out the door, grinning a devious grin. I shot him a one-fingered salute, about the only thing I could do at that point. I hope its meaning is as clear in Vietnam as in America.

Cindie pulled to a stop. She had been hit on her back, and was hurt more by the shock than by the missile, though it did leave a hefty welt.

"Let's keep riding," I said. "Injuries hurt less when you're moving".

She shot me a tearful look of anger, then she nodded. We started to ride, using the wonder of miles to put the incident behind us.

We were riding illegally these days – we had ridden past a police checkpoint where all the cops were sleeping. No one had hassled us about it, so we hoped that would continue until we were back in areas where permits were not needed.

Then as the afternoon went on we found ourselves in an

area of huge coffee plantations. This was a concern, because camping was illegal in this area and there was no place that we could hide. We were trying to reach the town of Pleiku, but it was too far for us to reach it on this day. What to do?

After riding for an hour, we saw a side road that headed through a plantation. Surely there would be a place down that road where we could hide ourselves for the evening. We turned down the dirt road, and found a place to put our tent up. As Cindie was taking a picture of me in the tent a man came upon us riding his bike.

"Uh, oh," Cindie told me. "He's seen us."

He certainly did. As soon as we made eye contact, he turned his bike around and pedaled the other way.

Was he getting the police? Or just scared of Westerners? We did not know, but we were undisturbed for the night.

Cindie ready to ride out of the coffee plantation.

Tim in our tent in the coffee plantation.

Chapter 9
Riding North

Vietnamese Funeral procession.

After our secretive night in the coffee plantation, we took our time. We knew we had a short day to reach Pleiku, so we slept late and relaxed over breakfast. Rural Vietnam gave us no reason to hurry.

Only a few minutes after we went back on the road, we witnessed a funeral. Dozens of men and women walked down the highway, carrying colorful banners on poles, and a box the size of a dog house, painted with green, purple and red designs. It would have been a festive sight, were it not for the weeping widow, who looked way too young – whoever had died must have been her age, and likely did not die from

Cindie meeting with local Vietnamese at an outdoor cafe.

natural causes.

We stopped for lunch a few kilometers from Pleiku and chatted with a nice family who happen to have an English/Vietnamese dictionary. It was fun learning Vietnamese with the kids.

As we sat eating lunch we saw three elephants go by. This was no show. A family of five was actually traveling by elephant, loaded on the back of the pachyderm (who, of course, had no trouble with such a light load). Amazing to think that such a sight exists in the 21st Century.

Pleiku is located in central Vietnam and is most known, at least to westerners, as a place that was heavily attacked by the Viet Cong during the war. It was the attack on this

168

city that prompted USA President Lyndon Johnson to begin a campaign of heavy bombing that further escalated the war.

When the region fell to the north, there was little left. After the war, the USSR helped to rebuild it ... and rather charmlessly too.

Still there was a hotel that accepted foreigners, which was good, although it charged a hefty US $12 for foreign tourists. We checked the hotel across the street and they wanted even more.

We went to bed early, tired from the heat. An hour after we had fallen asleep, the phone in our room rang and woke us up.

Cindie and I looked at each other. In all the hotel rooms we had stayed in the past two-and-a-half years of travel, we had never received a phone call. In fact, most hotel rooms did not even have phones.

Tentatively, I picked up the receiver: "Hello?"

"Hello," said a Vietnamese woman's accented voice on the other end. "Police want to know wha' you do tomorrow."

My first instinct was to say, "None of your business." Then I remembered we were in a Communist country. It was normal for the police to want to know what foreigners were doing – and the law gave them every right to ask.

"Hmmm," I said, trying to sound like I was searching my memory (in fact, I was trying to engage my groggy brain). "We haven't thought about it, really."

"That no good," she said. "Police must know wha' you do.

A magazine we found in our hotel room.

In this province police always want know where foreigner go."

"OK," I said, "We're going to stay in town and shop and

use the Internet café."

"You must tell if you are to change plans," she said. "Where you go next?"

"I don't know."

"Police say you no go to north," she told us. "You must go to coast."

Well, that was terrible news. Our plan had been to ride north on a dirt road through the remote highlands to Danang. That was our preference over the beaten track, which in this case was the busy and crowded Highway 1 along the coast. Though it looks like we were the beaten ones, unless we wanted to flaunt the law.

Not a good idea, we decided. Vietnamese authorities were not to be trifled with.

The next day we did laundry and went to the internet cafe. Where we learned our web site traffic was exploding but our server could not handle the increased volume, and consequently, was crashing and hurting our business. We half expected the police to show up and start questioning us. They never did, but we always had a feeling we were being watched.

Cindie wanted to take a bus out of here, to make sure the police did not bother us, but I talked her into riding out. As long as they saw us ride in the right direction, we should not have a problem.

The next morning, we were not confronted by the police as we left town. People seemed a little more edgy here and not used to foreigners. No one was sorry to see us go.

From Pleiku we rode east to An Khe, along a paved, hilly road surrounded by farms and pine trees. We had no information about the road ahead, and had no idea what to expect.

We crossed a high pass at noon, and down into a valley that felt like an inferno. It was so hot we stopped a couple of times to drink plenty of water. At one stop we watched hundreds of soldiers marching by. They were even herding cows along with the convoy. We wanted to take photos we knew that probably was not a good idea – it might be illegal.

From there, we climbed up another pass. This one was spotted with concrete bunkers built into the hillside, with horizontal slots facing the road.

"What are those?" Cindie asked.

"I think they're machine gun nests."

"You think there's anybody in them?"

"Naw," I said. "They were probably built during the war,"

Cindie shivered, thinking about soldiers keeping the enemy pinned down with cannon and gunfire. The American and South Vietnamese troops were massacred during a particularly nasty battle in this region during the war. A lot of blood was shed in this area.

Although we expected to camp out somewhere, we rode all the way to An Khe and found a hotel.

The benefit of heading from the highlands to the coast was it was mostly downhill. As we descended, the land turned from mountainous and dry to flat and very green.

We still had no idea where we were, at an outdoor café a local fellow stopped by on his bike. He wore an army green shirt and matching pants, and his teeth were yellow and stained from smoking. The bike he rode was like most of the bikes in Southeast Asia: a heavy one-speed with fenders and racks. In many places this would be the start of a wonderful conversation, given our recent experiences in Vietnam our suspicions were raised.

"You want cigarette?" he asked us, offering us one.

We both refused. I moved in close to Cindie's ear and said, "That is the oldest scam in the book. You take a cigarette and then he wants you to buy him a pack."

"Should we stay?" Cindie asked. At this point, we had not yet ordered.

"Maybe not," I said, waiting to see if he was going to be a pest.

"Give me water?" he demanded.

That was hard to say no to. We had a bottle of cold water from the restaurant, so I grabbed a new glass and poured him some.

"You buy cigarettes?" he asked. Apparently, he was not going away. So we paid for our water and got back on our bikes. So did he. He followed us, but did not keep up for long. His bike, though it lacked the heavy saddlebags that turned us into Lycra-clad water buffaloes, was still no match for our high-tech rides.

Eventually, we left him behind and rode at least 20 kilo-

Cyclist who followed us from restaurant to restaurant to hotel room.

Rice farmer working in the field.

meters (12 miles) to the intersection of Highway 1. When we found another nice restaurant, we sat down to eat again.

Soon, the cigarette guy showed up and joined us.

"No," we said. "You cannot sit here."

The restaurant owner chased him out. After we paid for our meals and left, we found him waiting for us across the street. We ignored him - what else could we do?

We biked half a kilometer down the road and stopped at a hotel. And as we were booking a room, our new best friend came in after us. This man was persistent. This time, the hotel staff chased him out. I wonder if he wanted us to take him all the way to Hanoi.

While the Vietnam coast may sound both scenic and exotic, the highway that follows it is anything but. The air horns on the buses and trucks could break an eardrum. The drivers are crazy or foolish. People stop in the middle of the road to unload a cart on a main highway. No one seems to acknowledge that in car-pedestrian accidents, the cars usually win.

Over the last week we noticed symbols of bikes painted on the road, and it was on this highway that I actually figured out what it meant: an accident scene where a bicyclist or motorcyclist was hit by a car.

The number of accidents on this road is staggering. If only people would look where they were going, there would be far fewer injuries and deaths.

Later on this highway I learned another secret of Vietnamese traffic: merging traffic does not yield to the main flow. It is the other way around. Merging traffic enters the main flow without stopping, and it is up to the rest of traffic to go around them. That makes it quite difficult for cyclists to merge, since we do not travel at car speed. The trick was to keep a steady pace, and everyone will go around. Or so we hoped.

We headed north, riding on a smooth, paved road with an ample shoulder. It was fairly flat, and would have been pleasant riding except for the noisy traffic.

The first day along the coast, heading to Sa Huynh, we were pleased to have a tailwind for nearly 80 kilometers (50 miles). We had heard the wind generally came from the north this time of year. Even though it was winter, the temperature was hot, and we stopped during the heat of the early afternoon for a cold drink and shade.

However, stopping was often frustrating. People were always touching our sweaty arms, which bothered Cindie more than me. The women especially seemed to be interested in me – always squeezing my arms, or poking me. Cindie thought I reminded these ladies of the soldiers who were here in the past.

In Su Huynh, we found a pleasant guesthouse. They even let us roll our bikes into our room, which was a nice change from leaving them with the scooters. We went to dinner at a restaurant nearby. There a man speaking fluent English came up to us and said he had been an interpreter for the Marines' Third Division."My family was taken away after the war," he said, "To a re-education camp..."

He was going to tell us more, but he was called away by a group of men. We were sorry to see him go– we really wanted to know more about the re-education camps and what took place there. I got the feeling he desperately wanted to tell us but it was obvious his friends did not want him talking to us.

The next day, as we continued our journey north toward Hanoi and the Chinese border, we hit our first big headwind in a while. It was a blustery morning, and got worse in the afternoon when it started raining hard along the flat road.

Tired, we sought shelter in a small café. Well, actually it was the owner's living room. The family was very inviting and made us tea and coffee and gave us cookies. To my surprise, Dad pulled out a large model airplane.

So, with smiles on our faces, we spent some time throwing airplanes around the living room, somehow avoiding all the lamps. How many people would do this with total strangers? We marveled.

While eating cookies, I looked around the small apartment. My eyes landed on a large shrine that took up about a quarter of the room. In the center were two faded photos, both young men. Paintings, lanterns and gifts surrounded the photos.

It was difficult to make out their faces through the incense smoke, still we were curious. I wanted to know the story behind these two. The mother noticed I was looking at the shrine. She started making gestures with her hands, and the meaning soon became clear.

Family who invited us out of the rain to have a cup of coffee and fly airplanes in their living room.

The lady of the house with a shrine to her brothers.

They were her two brothers, lost in the war (or a war, anyway, as it was not clear which one).

"Xin vui long (please)," she said, indicating we should take pictures of her with the shrine. We did.

The weather cleared, we said good bye to the family and we were traveling down the road again.

In Quang Ngai, we took a day off. It was raining all morning, and there seemed little reason to continue in such a downpour. The next day, we heard the man in the hotel room next to ours vomiting into the squat toilet. We did not think anything of it at the time, by mid-afternoon my wife knew how he felt. Apparently the food in the hotel where we stayed was not up to World Health Organization standards.

By dinner, Cindie was on a first-name basis with our privy. She had a fever and felt awful. This is the down side of adventure travel – you have to eat what the locals provide, and you are at their mercy. It was fortunate that this sort of malaise rarely hits us.

The next day, after a decent rest, Cindie's stomach felt like it wanted to be her friend again and we continued our journey. Road traffic was getting heavy, though at least the land – we were surrounded by rice paddies to the horizons– was flat and easy to pedal. We saw the result of another traffic accident, and were thankful that thus far we had not been so victimized. An otherwise-dull lunch turned serious when we realized, too late down the road, that we had left our map and guidebook behind. Now we really were sailing into unknown territory.

Lady selling rice cakes to Cindie.

Cindie buying vegetables at the open air market.

Tim in front of Japanese Friendship Bridge in Hoi An.

Riding through the streets of Hoi An.

Cindie buying baguettes from a street vendor.

In Hoi An, we found a pleasant town with ancient charm – narrow streets, vendors everywhere (and tourists, who are naturally drawn to this sort of thing). A few hours after checking into a hotel, we found a note on our door – it was Mary Ann, the American woman from the Jun village, she was staying at the same hotel and recognized our bikes in the lobby. She had just returned from the famed China Beach and was eager to catch up.

"How was China Beach?" Cindie asked her.

"Fantastic," Mary Ann said. She began to tell us about a place she found with cheap rooms and tasty (not to mention safe) food.

"Wow, we're heading there next," Cindie said. "How long

are you in town for?"

"A few more days. I found this great restaurant. Do you want to join me?"

"Sure," my wife said. "Let me see what time Tim wants to go eat."

"Wait. Are you busy now?"

"Why?"

"Well, Hoi An is famous for their tailors," Mary Ann said. "I had some custom-made travel pants done. I was about to go pick them up..."

"Really," said Cindie, her eyes lighting up. "Can you wait for me?"

Before I knew it, they were both gone, and I was left in the room by myself to work on the computer. The tailors of Hoi An, it seems, would have another customer.

The next day, we ran into an American couple who were also touring by bike – Linda and Jerry from Colorado. They were riding for a month, and quickly agreed to meet for dinner to compare stories about riding in Vietnam.

(Later on, we would hear about their trip through the Central Highlands. Unfortunately, Jerry was bitten by a monkey, and had to be rushed down to Ho Chi Minh City for a series of Rabies shots.)

Then it was our turn to go to China Beach. The Vietnamese name is My Khe, the English name stuck after American servicemen were helicoptered here for R&R during the war. The beach is the closest to Danang, a thriving city, and another well-known name from the war.

There was little at China Beach to remind us of military activities. The beach itself goes on for 30 kilometers (18 miles), and it was a desert of sand and surf. Except for a few fishing boats, there was little sign of any civilization. We stayed at the hotel recommended by Mary Ann called Hoa's Place, the only hotel we noticed. The owner charged US $7 a night, Vietnamese or Westerner.

Hoa was such a great host, and the beach was so nice, we decided to spend an extra night here. In the evenings, when tourists gathered at the small tables in the courtyard to eat dinner, Hoa was an attentive host, moving from group to group, trading small talk, doing card tricks, and asking questions of his visitors.

When he reached our table, we learned that Hoa, who spoke perfect English, was yet another person who worked as a translator for the Americans during the war. In fact, he and his wife had tried to escape the country when the North Vietnamese took over in 1975. He had very nearly gotten onto a boat, but his wife could not, so he stayed behind with her. They were both arrested and taken to a re-education camp. Many with ties to the South Vietnamese government toiled in places like that for as many as 10 years.

We asked Hoa what that was like. He smiled and coughed, and excused himself to say hello to another table. During our stay, Hoa would never discuss those years, and we soon learned not to ask. We can only imagine what it was like. This was another dark ghost of the American involvement – we

Tim, Cindie and Hoa at Hoa's Place.

Cindie looking in a fishing boat at China Beach.

could just flee back home when things got uncomfortable, leaving those who worked for us to face what the enemy had in store.

Cyclists start young in Vietnam.

Chapter 10
Hanoi Beckons, China looms

Two local girls wondering how heavy Cindie's bike is.

We were heading into the Northern part of Vietnam now, and the weather was turning cold, cloudy and damp. We were also planning to take a train to Hanoi – we concluded that our web site needed immediate attention because too much traffic was causing daily shut downs and strangling our business. My assignment in Vietnam's second-largest city would be to move all our data to a more robust server. Also, our three-month tourist visa was running out, and we wanted to make sure we had enough time to reach the border with China without any problems.

On the last day of riding before catching the train, I was in for a shock. I biked past a group of friendly boys, who wanted to say hello. When I slowed down to greet them, another kid picked up a sizable rock and hurled it at me. It hit me on the leg, and hurt quite a lot. The whole gang ran away.

I slammed on my brakes, changed directions, and pedaled after them. I did not put up with that kind of behavior when I was a teacher and I certainly was not going to now.

The boy's hair must have stood on end when he saw me coming - clearly he had not expected pursuit. He ran down an alley, doubling his speed, and I rode after him, ducking under laundry hanging from lines.

I followed that kid all the way to his hut, where he ran inside, terrified. I banged on the door, and when his mother came out I explained with hand motions what her son had done. His mother began to shout at her son; in what I'm sure was Vietnamese for "Just wait until your father gets home!"

We biked away, bewildered at such an unexpected show of hostility.

When we arrived in Hue (pronounced "Way"), we stayed at a hotel with the rare luxury of cable television. The first night, we were watching the BBC, lying in bed. We were fighting sleep, eyes closed, when something on the TV jerked us back to reality:

"...and in Thailand," went the British announcer, "a Swedish man has been arrested and charged with killing a local prostitute. Kenneth Eriksson, 40, was charged with beating and stabbing a woman in his hotel room in Pattaya, a popular Thai tourist destination, on February 15. Police said he later put the body in a duffel bag and tossed it over a nearby wall. He was caught on the hotel cameras dragging the heavy bag through the lobby ..."

"My God," Cindie said, staring at the small television screen. "It's him."

The TV showed a picture of the freakishly-pasty European who had sat down at our table in Pattaya a few months ago – the one who had obviously been partying nonstop for weeks. In the video, he was ducking from cameras and looking quite forlorn as the police dragged him from a car to a courtroom. When they showed his passport picture we knew it was definitely him.

Amazed, we watched the report. It seemed Eriksson had admitted to the killing, but said the girl had started it by stabbing him in the foot with a piece of glass while he was in the shower.

According to the report, Eriksson was a former Foreign Legionnaire and ice hockey referee, and had lived at the hotel for several months. He even gave a post-arrest interview with a Swedish newspaper which quoted him as saying: "I don't know how things got out of hand. What can I say? I guess it was because I'd been drinking and taking amphetamines. I don't know why the argument started in the first place."

"I knew he was trouble," I muttered as Cindie held her hand to her mouth.

After the body had been discovered, Eriksson fled to Bangkok, but was unable to leave Thailand because police were looking for him at the airports and land borders. The police contacted him by email. They reached out to his father, who also wrote him and suggested he give up. After two weeks on the run, he did, and was taken back to Pattaya for arraignment.

(Later he would be sentenced to five years in prison and in 2009; the case was reopened with Prosecutors seeking the death sentence.)

"You know," Cindie said as I turned off the TV. "I'm glad we never saw him again."

I nodded. "Me too."

Cindie was already feeling creeped out about this story when she lay down in bed and stared up at the ceiling. Then she screeched. "Tim, there's a giant spider right above me!"

I looked up. She was not kidding. It was bigger than my hand.

"I'll get it," I said, as I reached for my size 14 shoe.

"Wait a minute," Cindie said, calming down. "Let me get the camera."

The spider knew something was up, and was wary. When I took aim with the shoe, he skittered out of the way, a lot faster than I expected. He ran through a crack in the ceiling and disappeared.

"Oh, great," Cindie said. "Now we don't know where he is. I don't know if I can sleep here."

The monster spider we found in our room.

"You'll be fine," I said, reaching for the light switch. "Spiders are afraid of the dark."

"You're lying," she said as I got in bed beside her. "I hope he bites you first."

Fortunately, we never saw him again. I guess he did not take kindly to being threatened by such a large shoe.

We spent a few days in Hue before boarding the train to Hanoi. Hue is the former capital of the country, located

The Citadel in Hue.

Tim posing with local children.

near the coast and midway between Hanoi and Saigon. It's a peaceful city, full of vegetation, canals and lakes. It's got more of a French feel than other big cities here, and has five universities within its city limits.

The town has a number of historic points of interest, however, most of them are quite expensive to visit. We elected to visit its most popular place, the Citadel, where the dynasty of the Nguyen family ruled from 1744 to 1802. It's Vietnam's answer to China's famous Forbidden City, once home to their divine emperor.

At the Citadel, a visitor can spend hours, walking among the various buildings and imagining what life might have once been like for Vietnamese royals.

Hue, which is the closest big city to the former demilitarized zone line separating south from north, was heavily damaged during the Tet Offensive. Since then, the city has been rebuilt for visitors and it was nice to see it thriving. We knew we were in a tourist town again when the proprietor of our hotel set out to try to scam us when we checked out at 10 a.m.

The bill for our room was 364,000 dong, or US $30. Cindie laid out four crisp 100,000-dong notes and the clerk behind the desk gave her 36,000 dong for change. Cindie was about to walk away when the clerk said: "Hey, you no pay enough."

"What?"

"You pay 300,000 dong," he said, showing Cindie three bills. "You owe 100,000."

"I don't think so," Cindie said. "I paid you 400,000. Here's the change." She showed the man the 36,000 dong.

"You no can leave until you pay bill," he said, coming round from the back of the counter to confront Cindie.

At this point, I came down the stairs from our room, holding our bags. "This guy is trying to rip us off," she told me, explaining what was going on.

"What do you want to do?" I whispered.

"He thinks we're in a hurry," she said. "He knows we have a train to catch."

"We do."

"Yeah, but we've got plenty of time. Let's wait him out."

Cindie looked up at the man, who was watching us expectantly. "We'll wait until you find the money," she said, and we both sat down on a nearby bench. His face fell.

Fifteen minutes later, he came running over. "I look and find the money," he said. "No problem."

Cindie smiled sweetly. "I knew you would."

At the station, we checked our bikes into the baggage car and made our way to the sleepers. Cindie did not enjoy the ride. It turned out she was the only woman in the sleeping car. All the men on this train traveled in first class, while their wives and children were forced to stay in the cheaper second-class seats. It's times like this that we realize how far women's rights have come in the USA and how far they have to go in places like Vietnam. After a continent of *machismo* in Latin America, we were used to it, still it bugged us – espe-

Cindie with the Internet Cafe owner in Hanoi.

cially Cindie. We knew there would be plenty more countries where we would see similarly-ugly social norms.

Stepping off the train into Hanoi, we could feel the vibe of the city. It had been several weeks since we had been to Ho Chi Minh City, and we felt out of place in this urban maelstrom. Retrieving our bikes from the baggage car, we rode carefully down the busy avenues of the Old City, buzzing with business and busy-ness. It was a relief to get off the

Water Puppet show in Hanoi.

Musicians at the Water Puppet show.

street to find a hotel, and refuge.

Hanoi is to the north as Ho Chi Minh City (Saigon) is to the south. Despite the hectic life we experienced on our first ride here, Hanoi is far more relaxed than its southern neighbor. Where Saigon is the gateway to the southern flatlands of the Mekong Delta, Hanoi is the gateway to the world of northern Vietnam, a place of vegetation-covered karst towers and tribal villages of ethnic minorities.

Our main purpose here was not to explore, but to fix our web site by moving all our data to a new server. It would be a process that would take days and days, especially on the slow connections in this part of the world.

So I settled into a 10-day residency at the nearest internet café, while Cindie explored the city and made plans for us to visit some of the better sights when I was done. One night we went to see a performance of water puppets, a small theater where the puppets perform over a tank of water. The most unusual attraction was the embalmed body of Ho Chi Minh himself.

Still referred to as "Uncle Ho" by foreign tourists; the revered leader of Vietnamese independence never wanted to be a tourist attraction. Ho Chi Minh led the country to independence from the French, only to watch his people descend into a civil war made worse by foreign manipulation. Not only was he not able to achieve the unity he sought, he could not even get the death he wanted. He asked for a simple funeral and cremation. Instead, he got pickled.

To see his body, you have to wait in line for hours, surrounded by Vietnamese patriots looking somber, hats in hands and carrying flowers. Cameras are not allowed inside the tomb. Ho Chi Minh lies in a casket of gold and glass, visible to all (except for two months a year, when he's sent to Moscow for refurbishment). It was a strange and morbid sight. When we were finished, we had to walk through a museum and tacky gift shop selling Ho Chi Minh buttons and flags.

Cindie used her free time in Hanoi to learn more about Vietnamese culture – people in Hanoi were workhorses.

"They are very tenacious," she reported to me one night. "Right at the crack of dawn, every single shop door opens, and they start working immediately. And they work hard until the end of the day."

Whole streets in the old city were dedicated to a single trade – tailors, basket makers, carpet makers, butchers, bakers all had their own block. Thanks to the French, there were tasty baguettes everywhere, and sweeping French architecture the likes of which we had not seen before in this country.

Of course, we experienced the usual two-tiered pricing system. At one restaurant, where we must have eaten four times, we were charged a different price every day, even though we ordered the same thing each time.

And there was other weirdness. At one point, a man came up and asked me in Vietnamese for my shoes. Really. He pointed at my feet and made it very clear what he wanted.

I just laughed. I have no idea what he wanted with them – probably as a gag to show his friends. Vietnamese feet are much smaller than Western feet. Especially mine.

We also found a bootleg DVD/CD shop near our hotel. It was the first time we really understood how prevalent the bootleg industry was. The shop was in the tourist district, and most of the customers were westerners, paying US $1 for the latest movies. Had we wanted to, we could have watched all the Oscar-nominated movies on DVD before they had been officially released in the states.

We experienced price-gouging everywhere – worse than any other city we have seen. A bag of popcorn was four times the local price for westerners, and the seller refused to come down, even when we walked away. A motorcycle driver would agree to a round-trip fare, only to announce at the end of our trip that the price was for one way and each person. Bargaining in most places is fun – in Hanoi we experienced nothing but anger that a tourist would dare question their being ripped off. It was very disheartening.

In the meantime, Cindie ran into Mary Ann again. One weekend, they went to visit a hill town outside the city, called Bac Ha. The village is in the mountains, close to better-known Sapa and the Chinese border. It's famous for its Sunday market, and is a great place to people-watch.

Mary Ann and Cindie took the train north, and then negotiated for a ride on the back of a motorcycle. They arrived on Saturday afternoon and stayed for the night. Large speakers were set up on telephone poles around town, and the

Young girls with their babies gathered at the Sunday market near Bac Ha.

Women selling bowls of rice and noodles at the market near Bac Ha.

Young girl waiting for her mom to finish shopping.

A woman smoking tobacco out of a bong at the market.

Little girls playing at the Bac Ha market.

announcements broadcast at crushing volume kept them up well into the night. They did not know if they were spouting propaganda or advertising.

The market, Cindie reported, was well worth the trip. Local tribes women dressed in brightly colored skirts and shirts, with babies tied to their back, bargained hard in local tongues. The men wore mostly black and sat together in dining areas while their wives conducted business. The men ate bowls of pig's blood, apparently a local delicacy that Cindie declined to try.

After I finished the work on the computer, we mounted up our bikes and cycled north out of the city. Traffic was nowhere near as difficult as in Ho Chi Minh City (Saigon). We crossed the languid Red River on a railroad bridge, using lanes set up for local bike traffic. A pleasant path filled with locals on one-speed steel bikes went another three kilometers (1.8 miles) before we rejoined the road. It was good to be on the bike again.

We were getting close to China now – only a few more days. The first night after Hanoi, in Bac Giang, we found a nice hotel. Cindie bought a kilo (2.2 lbs.) of oranges for the equivalent of 50 cents, about one-third the price in Hanoi. Then she noticed the meat vendors. And saw the head of an animal she had never seen in a market before.

It was a dog. Her stomach did flips. It may be considered a local delicacy in this part of the world, that's one cultural leap Cindie is not willing to make. We soon learned to avoid restaurants serving "thit cho," the word for cooked dog.

The next two days it rained a light drizzle, making the dirt roads muddy and wet. The locals carried umbrellas, and were surprised to see us pedaling through the dampness. Our formerly-clean bikes soon looked like they had been riding through rice paddies. While the riding was not the most pleasant we ever had, the karst towers took our breath away. These giant limestone cliffs go up at least 90 meters (300 feet), and in the mist of the rainy season stand out like shadowy sentinels.

Only two days to the border now. My stomach was cramping, the results of something I had eaten, no doubt. We had other worries, too. China was coming. It gave us pause.

We knew so little about the most populous country in the world. We had heard it was a hard country for visitors to travel through. Few people outside the cities speak English. The police are everywhere, more like Big Brother than in any other nation, and they are deeply suspicious of westerners. We had a three-month tourist visa, and planned to have it extended for as long as possible. What if we weren't successful?

As China approached, our minds reflected back to our time in Southeast Asia. When we left Hanoi, we also celebrated the third anniversary of our life on the road. So much had changed since we first left Prescott, Arizona and pedaled south. I remembered how Cindie trembled as we first set off, the comments of some of our doubting friends – "You cannot ride a bike through these dangerous countries" – echoing through our heads.

We had certainly proved them wrong, so far at least.

The doubters' tunes soon changed from "you're going to get killed" to "you're going to go broke." We proved that wrong too. Our new, improved web site was working better than ever, and our book was selling well.

We kept biking, passing two men fighting over a motor-cycle accident. Later, another man on a bike caught up to us, then gave us a long speech in Vietnamese that neither of us had a hope of understanding. These things might have fazed us only a few months before, now did not bother us at all.

I often say to Cindie when confronted with a particularly difficult situation: "Ain't no beginners here." I don't feel that we are experts either. We are still learning something new every day. To survive on the road takes common sense, adapt-ability, and the willingness to accept things that we do not understand or agree with. It takes letting go of everything we know and just going with the flow. I can imagine that Marco Polo knew this too, and repeated a 13th Century version of "Go with the flow" all the way to Mongolia.

Our three-year anniversary caused us to talk for days about what this trip means to us, and how we keep changing because of it. In the grey drizzle that followed us for days out of Vietnam and into China, we came to several conclusions:

Our time in the saddle has made some things easier, like choosing equipment, packing every day, and adjusting to endless foreign cultures. Yet it has not taken away the new-ness and excitement. We have not become jaded. Every day we experience something different and have an opportunity

Having our bikes washed in preparation for crossing the Chinese border.

to learn about the countries we visit and the people we meet. It is endlessly rewarding and there is nothing that we would rather be doing. We are both committed to circling the globe until we are physically unable to continue. We still have a long, long way to go.

Before the Chinese border, we stopped at a motorcycle washing station, to clean off our bikes. Then we changed into fresh clothes. We had learned from our many international border crossings that things go smoother when you look neat and clean. As we were waiting in line to get stamped out of Vietnam, a foreign guy who was riding the bus apparently over stayed his visa. The police dragged him into a back room – no doubt to force him to pay a hefty fine or worse. The Vietnamese border guards were serious. They scrutinized our passports, stamped our visas with an exit date and sent us through.

On April 3, 2005, with heart's pumping, we pedaled across no man's land and up to Chinese border officials. A new road was beginning.

Tim riding towards the Chinese border.

Epilogue
Dreaming of an Endless Bicycle Tour

Bicycle touring is magical; anyone who has ventured off on two wheels has felt it. Few activities combine the benefits of exercise with the excitement of travel and personal growth. These special feelings are as individual as the people riding their silent machines on the back roads of the globe. A common denominator has to be the feeling of freedom; where life is boiled down to its simplest of terms. Only a few possessions can be carried so there is less to worry about. A steaming plate of spaghetti by a campfire is more enjoyable than an expensive night out on the town. Spring cleaning is riding in the rain. Keeping up with fashion is remembering to put on a different shirt every day. On a bike tour stress melts away and life is beautiful.

I have absolutely loved the simplicity and freedom of my own tours. My only complaint was not flat tires or rain but instead every tour ended and I had to return to a mainstream life. At first I went through withdrawals but eventually a monotonous daily routine was reestablished and another journey entered the planning stages. Working and saving money, even if it took many years, was just an intermission to my episodes of really living life. It was like listening to a radio station that ran 95% commercials while the remaining 5% played my favorite song. I have experienced these highs and lows far too many times but felt powerless to do anything about it. Many years would pass before I discovered a way to endlessly ride my bike throughout the world.

I have to go back in time to explain how this happened. I met my wife Cindie in 1995 while attending graduate school at Northern Arizona University in Flagstaff, Arizona. We had a two-wheeled romance; our first date was a mountain bike ride which led to more cycling outings.

Two years later our relationship changed when Cindie expressed an interest in buying a tandem with me. At that moment I knew, as a life long cyclist, this was the ultimate sign of commitment, when a couple buys a tandem it means they plan to ride together for life. It was time to ask her to marry me.

I proposed during a bike ride by simply pulling up next to her and nervously asking, "Will you ride with me the rest of your life; will you marry me?"

She answered, "Yes, if you can catch me" and shifted up and sprinted away.

We were married in a Las Vegas drive thru called, "The Tunnel of Love." The ceremony consisted of us riding up on single bikes, the Justice of the Peace spoke, and we switched to our brand new tandem and rode away. We have been joined in this symbolic way ever since.

A few years later after we had settled into our working and married life, I was dreaming of another trip but this time one of grand proportions. Talking Cindie into giving up her successful career, comfortable house, and committing to a multi-year bicycle tour was not easy but on March 30, 2002

210

we set off to peddle our way around the world. At this point in time I still saw my bike tours as temporary so, for our trip, we estimated we had saved enough money to travel cheaply for seven years. This was a huge adjustment for a couple who had professional jobs. To stay in budget, we learned to copy the habits of locals by eating where they ate, shopping in open air markets and staying in the same hotels as truck drivers. Between cities we became experts at finding hidden places on the side of the road to free camp for the night.

The first year we traveled from Arizona through Mexico, Guatemala, Honduras, Nicaragua, Costa Rica and Panama. The second year we traveled through Ecuador, Peru, Bolivia, Argentina and Chile. It was the most free I had ever felt and I was intoxicated with it.

During the initial months of the trip we defined our journey in terms of stamps in our passports, miles ridden and drawing a line on a map. It didn't take long to embrace the deeper rewards of travel; spending time with locals and observing how they live. For example, being invited into a family's home because we looked wet, cold and lost was a journey deep into the religions, traditions and food customs of the region. What they cooked and how they ate told volumes more about their lives than taking pictures out of a bus window. Traveling on a bicycle placed us on the ground floor of society but that was not enough. In order to absorb the culture around us, it was just as important to have time off the bikes as time in the saddle. Riding bicycles became a means of meeting people rather than a goal in itself. Interacting with locals reduced our daily mileage but we gladly made the trade. We did not care about the fastest route but instead chose a route well off the beaten track that guaranteed immersion into the colorful cultures that define each region.

At the end of the second year I could not escape the thought that I only had a few years left of freedom. I should have been happy with the remaining time instead I was scared. This magical feeling had an ending point just like my previous trips. We would eventually have to return home and save up for another adventure.

Cindie also loved life on the road with its daily discoveries and endless opportunities to learn and grow. These two years pushed her passed the point of no return and she didn't want our trip to end either. We repeatedly asked each other, "How can we sustain our travels while living on the road?" As with every challenge we faced we worked together as a team and looked for the answer.

Like many other bike tourists we tossed around the idea of creating a book. I was regularly writing for our web site and enjoyed expressing myself in this way and it seemed to be a logical progression. When we asked others, who had written similar books, about it's feasibility, we were discouraged to hear horror stories of stacks of unsold books, lost investments and were consistently advise not to attempt it. We were told, "Having a good story to tell in an entertaining way is not enough. The book has to be sold in high enough numbers to make it economically viable". Discouraged, we looked elsewhere for solutions.

While in Latin America, we came across a few travelers who played guitar with a hat out or sold handmade jewelry on the street, some of the most interesting drifters we had met. They had guts, faith, or something special because they appeared to be just scraping by and yet didn't have a care in the world. I admired their creativity and tenacity to stay on the road. Cindie and I had none of these skills. We don't sing, play instruments, or make crafts. We had to find our own answer to our puzzling question of sustainable travel.

Instead of thinking of what we couldn't do we forced ourselves to think outside the box and focused on what we could do. When we thought about it, our web site, www.DownTheRoad.org, received thousands of visitors each month and was similar to publishing a small magazine.

The question changed to, "How do we sustain our travels utilizing the internet and our web site?" We often traveled in places where electricity and internet was scarce. Despite these limitations an internet based solution still held promise. We found ways to sell advertising on our web site which led to a small but growing income. We were on the right track and knew we just had to open our minds a little more and see what else was outside the box.

We sold third party books through an online bookstore' commission sales program from our web site. Even though the commissions didn't add up to much we were surprised to see the total number of books we sold each month was in the hundreds. Our thoughts returned to writing our own book and selling it directly from our web site. Inside the box we were afraid to create a book because of the failures of others but outside the box we knew we were different. We had a busy web site to generate interest in our story. This meant a book could not only be fun to write and provide a wonderful creative outlet but could also be profitable enough to sustain our travels.

Cindie and I agreed that we could not bare another trip ending and decided to, once again, chase a seemingly impossible dream and self publish a book about our travels. Working together and overcoming all of the challenges we faced while traveling through Latin America was our source of confidence to jump into this huge project because we knew, as a team, we could do anything we set our minds to. To publish a book we had to take a substantial gamble with our remaining travel funds. If our book failed financially we would have to go home early but if it was successful we could earn a tour of the globe that never had to end. It was a gamble that translated to how much or how little of the world we could see. We worked hard to write, edit and publish our first book, *The Road That Has No End* and our dream of endless travel was on its way to turning into a reality.

After South America and the release of our first book, we toured Thailand, Cambodia, Vietnam, a nine month loop in China, Laos and back to Thailand. Next, we took a four month rest in Malaysia where we started work on our second book, before we continued on to Singapore, a year tour in Australia and eight months in New Zealand where we took

214

a two month break to edit our second book and enjoy the countryside. Then we flew to Alaska and finalized and published our second book, *Down the Road in South America* before riding to the lower forty eight and a sixteen month tour of the USA and Canada. We spent winter 2010 in Indiana with family and completed our third book, *Down the Road in Thailand, Cambodia and Vietnam*. The following spring, we flew to India to continue our journey.

While cycling in Australia and New Zealand, some five years after we started the trip, our web site traffic and book sales grew and we started breaking even financially. Our temporary tour evolved into a perpetual bicycle touring lifestyle and the fear of the trip ending was gone. I finally found the radio station that plays my favorite song non stop and all I want to do is turn it up loud and enjoy every minute of it.

In the future we plan on visiting all the bike-able places we have not explored yet including, but not in order, Japan, Central Asia, Russia, The Middle East, Europe, Africa and more. Along the way there will be more books and there is even talk of a DVD movie project. We have no plans to stop traveling, writing and exploring new opportunities!

Obviously, traveling this many years is having profound effects on us but not in ways many would think. These changes are not static but are instead happening slowly, as we experience more of the world and constantly reevaluate our values. Peering deep into ourselves is the true journey instead of the superficial line we draw on a map.

When we were on temporary trips the simplicity and freedom of a bike tour was a vacation from our regular lives of working and surviving the rat race. Looking back at the years leading up to our departure we wonder how we juggled all the complexities of modern life. There were bills to pay, cars to fix, schedules to keep, bosses to impress and a million other things to get done before the end of the day, month, or year. We used to say, "There isn't enough hours in a day to do all the things that need to get done." Now we have far less things to worry about and feel like we have all day to see what will come our way. After several years of living a simple life on bikes with our possessions being limited to what can be carried we have evolved into a very simplistic yet open minded way of looking at life. Everything is beautiful in its own basic way and the great weight of worry and stress has been lifted from our shoulders. We are free to explore, learn and drift.

This many years on the road have taught Cindie and me to throw away the big list of things we would like to own and be content with what we have. We now find happiness in the simple pleasures of life and don't seek our identities in the things we own. It sounds so simple and idealistic but the results have been monumental.

You can experience the places we have been to with thousands of pictures, Cindie's daily journal, videos and learn how our future travels unfold by visiting our web site www.DownTheRoad.org

Appendix A
Equipment List

Our fully loaded touring bikes.

This equipment list contains the gear we use while bike touring in general and is not specific to Southeast Asia. In Southeast Asia you could easily leave cold weather clothing and camping gear like a tent, sleeping bag, stove, pots and pans at home. However, we carried these items because we knew we would be camping in various regions of China and beyond. We shared items whenever possible.

<u>Bicycles</u> - Two touring bikes: each with 26-inch wheels, front and rear racks, bike computers, bells, water bottles, cages, tail lights, kickstands, touring saddles and clipless pedals.

<u>Panniers</u> - (bike saddlebags) Front and rear waterproof panniers, seat bags, handlebar bags and repair kit. We use adjustable bungee cords to hold the tent, sleeping bags, and pads on top of our rear racks.

Tim waking up in our tent.

Our gasoline burning stove.

Camping for Two

- tent and repair kit
- tent stakes
- ground cloth
- light weight tarp (used to cover the bikes)
- sleeping bags and water-proof dry bag stuff sacks
- sleeping pads with camp chair attachment

Water Purification and Storage

- 10 liter (2.6 gallon) water storage bag/solar shower
- 3 bicycle water bottles (each)
- 0.2 micron ceramic water filter and repair kit
- iodine tablets

Stove

- gasoline burning camp stove
- wind screen
- lighter
- cleaning and repair kit
- fuel bottle (size varies)

Kitchen Utensils

- cooking knife
- small flexible cutting board
- can opener (army style)
- spices: salt, pepper, garlic, cinnamon, ginger and more
- olive oil
- resealable bags
- dish drying cloth

Food Staples

- coffee
- sweetener
- powdered milk
- peanut butter
- bread or tortillas
- oatmeal
- pasta and sauce
- rice
- fresh, canned or dried vegetables
- instant noodles
- canned meat
- powdered soup

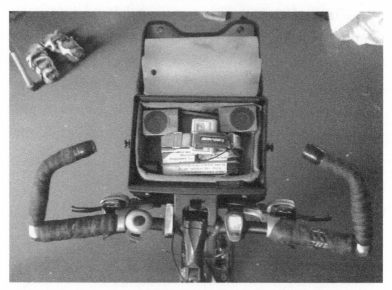

MP3 player and amplified speakers in Tim's handlebar bag.

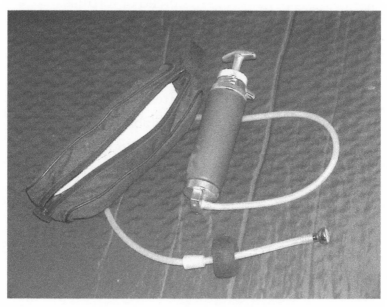

0.2 micron ceramic water filter.

Electronics

- laptop computer and power cord
- network cable
- MP3 player
- external amplified speakers
- headphones
- AM/FM shortwave radio

Camera

-video/still camera
- extra high capacity battery
- connector cables
- power cord for charging
- lens cleaning kit
- zoom, wide angle, polarized and UV lens

- mini tripod
- extra flash memory

Power and Electricity

- AA rechargeable batteries (several)
- AA battery charger and cord
- extension cord with three way splitter (US plugs)
- international plug adaptors
- light socket adaptor (T)

Other Electronics

- flash light/head lamps
- altimeter/compass watch

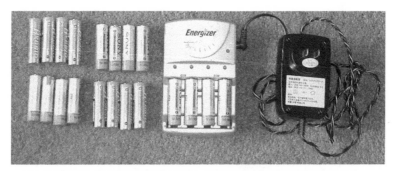

Battery charger and AA rechargeable batteries.

Our pots and pans fit into the largest pan.

T Adaptor converts a light socket into an electrical outlet.

First Aid Kit

- international health and first aid manual
- adhesive bandages (various sizes)
- elastic-wrap bandage
- gauge, pads and roll
- antiseptic wipe
- safety pins
- medical tape
- folding scissors
- tweezers
- antibacterial cream
- burn/first aid cream
- antifungal cream
- eye drop antibiotic
- aspirin/ibuprofen
- antihistamine
- moleskin
- antacid tablets

Antibiotics

- Doxycycline (Malaria)
- Metronidazole (for Amoebiasis and Giardiasis)
- Ciprofloxacin (for Bacillary Dysentery, Shigellosis)
- Amoxycillin (for broad spectrum for general use such as infected cuts)
- Mebendazole (for worms)
- thermometer

Health

- lip balm
- sunscreen
- insect repellent and mosquito coils
- multivitamins
- earplugs
- eye mask (blindfold for sleeping)

Toiletries

- toilet paper
- toothbrush and toothpaste
- quick drying towel
- brush/comb
- shampoo and conditioner
- bar soap
- razor
- fingernail clippers
- small mirror

Folding spare tires are small and can be a life saver in remote areas.

Cindie camping in Inner Mongolia, China.

Cycling Clothing
(per person)

- 2 cycling shorts
- 1 or 2 short sleeve jerseys
- 1 wool long sleeve jersey
- 1 cycling tights
- 1 pair cycling gloves
- helmet
- sunglasses
- bandana

Off Bike Clothing
(per person)

- 2 short sleeve shirt
- 2 convertible shorts/pants
- 4 pairs lightweight wool socks
- swimsuit
- sun hat
- underwear
- laundry bags used to separate clothing in our panniers
- sewing repair kit

Cold Weather Gear
(per person)

- fleece jacket
- long underwear top
- long underwear bottom
- mid-layer/wool long-sleeved top
- cold weather hat
- long fingered gloves

Rain Gear (per person)

- wind/rain jacket
- waterproof socks
- waterproof helmet covers

Shoes (per person)

- bike shoes
- walking shoes
- sandals

Documents and Money

- money belt
- credit card/s
- ATM debit card/s
- travelers checks
- small calculator
- local currency
- emergency stash of $US
- maps
- travel/guide books
- passports/visas/permits
- copies of documents
- vaccination records
- driver's licenses
- small note pad and pen

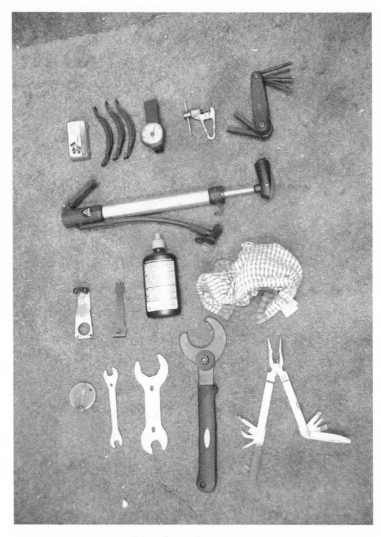

Bicycle tools we carry.

Security

- combination padlock for hostel lockers
- combination cable lock for bikes

Tools (carried between us)

- patch kit
- tire levers
- tire pump
- tire pressure gauge
- chain tool
- allen key set
- cassette cracker (remover)
- chain ring bolt wrench
- cone wrench if not using sealed cartridge hubs
- chain lube/rag
- spoke wrench
- 8 and 10 mm wrench
- pedal/32 mm headset wrench if not using threadless system
- crank puller/bottom bracket tool
- multi tool/knife - (blade, pliers, screwdrivers, needle nose pliers, file etc.)

Spare parts and repair kits

- one folding spare tire
- spare tubes (number depends on the continent)
- shift/brake cable
- shift/brake cable housing
- spare brake pads
- spare spokes
- bike grease
- frame bolts
- short chain replacement section with extra joining links
- electrical tape
- zip ties

Other

- laundry cord and detergent
- pillow
- mini binoculars
- recreational reading books
- local language/English dictionary
- reading glasses

Cindie in Cambodia on her loaded touring bike.

Camping by the Murray River in Australia.

Our Books

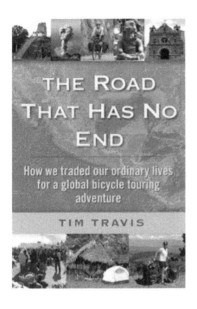 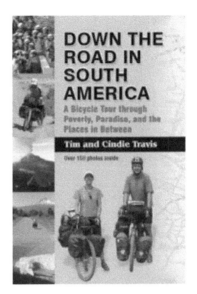

*The Road That Has No End: How we Traded our Ordinary Lives
for a Global Bicycle Touring Adventure*

ISBN: 978-9754427-0-8

*Down The Road in South America: A Bicycle Tour Through
Poverty , Paradise, and the Places in Between*

ISBN: 978-9754427-3-9

Available in Paperback, eBook, and audio book at our web
site: www.DownTheRoad.org

Lightning Source UK Ltd.
Milton Keynes UK
UKHW012013181120
373645UK00001B/72